D1074454

CHICAGO PUBLIC LIBRARY

Responding to the Needs of Today's Minority Students

Doris J. Wright, *Editor*
University of Texas at Austin

NEW DIRECTIONS FOR STUDENT SERVICES
MARGARET J. BARR, *Editor-in-Chief*
Texas Christian University

M. LEE UPCRAFT, *Associate Editor*
Pennsylvania State University

Number 38, Summer 1987

Paperback sourcebooks in
The Jossey-Bass Higher Education Series

Jossey-Bass Inc., Publishers
San Francisco • London

Doris J. Wright (ed.).
Responding to the Needs of Today's Minority Students.
New Directions for Student Services, no. 38.
San Francisco: Jossey-Bass, 1987.

LC
3731
.R36
1987

New Directions for Student Services
Margaret J. Barr, *Editor-in-Chief;* M. Lee Upcraft, *Associate Editor*

Copyright © 1987 by Jossey-Bass Inc., Publishers
and
Jossey-Bass Limited

Copyright under International, Pan American, and Universal
Copyright Conventions. All rights reserved. No part of
this issue may be reproduced in any form—except for brief
quotation (not to exceed 500 words) in a review or professional
work—without permission in writing from the publishers.

New Directions for Student Services is published quarterly
by Jossey-Bass Inc., Publishers (publication number USPS
494-090). Second-class postage paid at San Francisco, California, and at
additional mailing offices. POSTMASTER: Send address changes to
Jossey-Bass Inc., Publishers, 433 California Street, San Francisco,
California 94104.

Editorial correspondence should be sent to the Editor-in-Chief,
Margaret J. Barr, Sadler Hall, Texas Christian University,
Fort Worth, Texas 76129.

783 47311

Library of Congress Catalog Card Number LC 85-644751

International Standard Serial Number ISSN 0164-7970

International Standard Book Number ISBN 1-55542-971-8

Cover art by WILLI BAUM

Manufactured in the United States of America

Ordering Information

The paperback sourcebooks listed below are published quarterly and can be ordered either by subscription or single copy.

Subscriptions cost $48.00 per year for institutions, agencies, and libraries. Individuals can subscribe at the special rate of $36.00 per year *if payment is by personal check.* (Note that the full rate of $48.00 applies if payment is by institutional check, even if the subscription is designated for an individual.) Standing orders are accepted.

Single copies are available at $11.95 when payment accompanies order. (California, New Jersey, New York, and Washington, D.C., residents please include appropriate sales tax.) For billed orders, cost per copy is $11.95 plus postage and handling.

Substantial discounts are offered to organizations and individuals wishing to purchase bulk quantities of Jossey-Bass sourcebooks. Please inquire.

Please note that these prices are for the academic year 1986–87 and are subject to change without notice. Also, some titles may be out of print and therefore not available for sale.

To ensure correct and prompt delivery, all orders must give either the *name of an individual* or an *official purchase order number.* Please submit your order as follows:

Subscriptions: specify series and year subscription is to begin.
Single Copies: specify sourcebook code (such as, SS1) and first two words of title.

Mail orders for United States and Possessions, Latin America, Canada, Japan, Australia, and New Zealand to:
Jossey-Bass Inc., Publishers
433 California Street
San Francisco, California 94104

Mail orders for all other parts of the world to:
Jossey-Bass Limited
28 Banner Street
London EC1Y 8QE

New Directions for Student Services Series
Margaret J. Barr, *Editor-in-Chief;* M. Lee Upcraft, *Associate Editor*

SS1   *Evaluating Program Effectiveness,* Gary R. Hanson
SS2   *Training Competent Staff,* Ursula Delworth
SS3   *Reducing the Dropout Rate,* Lee Noel

Contents

Editor's Notes

Most colleges and universities have programs for recruitment and retention of ethnic minority students. Although programs vary in content, scope, and depth (depending on the parent institutions' commitment to minority student support services), most emphasize academic support and social adjustment, as well as recruitment and retention.

Unfortunately, institutional support for minority services and activities reached its height during the early 1970s. Since that time, enrollment of minority students has decreased in some institutions; others have decided to consolidate, reduce, or eliminate minority support programs and services. While these changes may be directly attributable to reductions in federal and state financial support for minority student programs, the institutions themselves are reneging on their commitment to support minority students through comprehensive programs and services.

As will be seen throughout this sourcebook, there is increasing anecdotal and statistical evidence that minority students' academic success in college is linked to certain emotional, social, and academic supports, as well as to positive campus environmental factors that encourage and challenge minority students to achieve. Institutions that are most successful in graduating minority students have developed programs and services not only to meet the needs of minority students but also to affect other college students, staff, faculty, and the administration through positive endorsement of cultural and academic diversity. In short, the successful programs and services ensure minority students' success and educate others about the values associated with a culturally diverse campus.

The purpose of this sourcebook is to provide student affairs practitioners with knowledge and methods for developing comprehensive, effective services and programs to enhance recruitment and retention and to facilitate the personal growth of ethnic minority students. The contributing authors have outlined several innovative programs and offer suggestions to assist practitioners in serving minority students more effectively. Most important, this sourcebook provides a framework for planning and implementing comprehensive programs for minorities in predominantly white institutions and gives direction to institutions for the twenty-first century.

In the first chapter, Doris J. Wright outlines the societal context in which ethnic minority students first entered predominantly white institutions and then examines minority students' developmental needs, as understood by current theory.

Augustine W. Pounds discusses the needs of black college students in Chapter Two. No longer are black students a singular, homogeneous group; rather, they are heterogeneous and, as such, require creative programming strategies to respond to their academic and social support needs.

Ethnic, social, and cultural diversity are watchwords that characterize Asian American college students. Charlene A. Chew and Alan Yoshiharu Ogi, in Chapter Three, highlight the challenges of providing services to this exciting group. They go far to eradicate the notion of Asians as a "successful minority" and offer practical suggestions for working with this group, whose social and academic needs will expand in the future.

In Chapter Four, Ennio L. Quevedo-García dispels myths about U.S. Hispanics, pointing out that they are heterogeneous, representing distinct countries of origin. Among the fastest-growing populations, Hispanics pose to institutions the challenge of recognizing their linguistic, cultural, academic, and social developmental needs. Several strategies for working with Hispanic students are presented.

Chapter Five demonstrates the difficulties institutions encounter in retaining American Indian students. Deborah Wetsit LaCounte presents an excellent analysis of American Indian college students and outlines several key ingredients for conducting successful Native American programs.

In Chapter Six, W. Terrell Jones discusses past and present conditions of minority-white peer interactions in white institutions. Included are examples and strategies for improving minority-white student interactions in the future.

In Chapter Seven, Doris J. Wright reviews the various issues and strategies for working effectively with minority students, recommends future directions for practitioners, and presents annotated references for use in program planning.

An appendix offers guidelines and standards for minority student services and programs.

Readers should recognize that the term *minority* is commonly used to identify U.S. ethnic minority groups that are underrepresented politically, economically, or socially, or groups that by legislation or social custom have been denied full access to higher education. While we recognize that there is much debate regarding the legitimacy and appropriateness of this term, we have chosen it to simplify mutual recognition of U.S. ethnic minority groups. The term *minority* is intended not to imply a status that is lower than any other group's but rather to describe a group's numerical representation in the U.S. population.

This sourcebook would not have been possible without the support of the Counseling and Mental Health Center at The University of Texas at Austin. More specifically, special thanks go to the clerical staff: Victoria

Barnaart, Sidney Brammer, Frances Logue, Mary Lou Lumpe, and Kristi Whitson. Jackie Masters deserves special appreciation for her editorial refinements, and Shirley Lott for her administrative assistance.

Doris J. Wright
Editor

Doris J. Wright is a staff psychologist at the Counseling and Mental Health Center at the University of Texas at Austin. Since 1970, she has worked with minority students on six campuses. She writes frequently on minority student development.

America's ethnic minorities challenge student affairs institutions and professionals to understand how minorities best flourish.

Minority Students: Developmental Beginnings

Doris J. Wright

America's ethnic minorities have sought involvement in colleges and universities since the beginning of the republic. Their struggle for entry into college was and still is a struggle for freedom—a fight inherent in American and especially collegiate American ideals of liberty and justice.

This chapter discusses the entry of American ethnic minorities into higher education, especially in predominantly white universities, and describes the developmental needs of minority college students. With this developmental framework comes a clearer, more revealing portrait of minority students' college years.

No Land of Opportunity

America in the early days was a land of opportunity, where success was open to any and all who worked hard and possessed strong achievement and entrepreneurial skills, ambition, and ingenuity (Astin, 1982). Contemporary America has extended and expanded upon those earlier work-ethic ideals. Today the United States can be described as a highly technological and credential-oriented society, in which anyone possessing a bright analytical mind, hard-driving ambition, the finest technological resources, a college degree, and an edge on the market will succeed.

D. J. Wright (ed.). *Responding to the Needs of Today's Minority Students.*
New Directions for Student Services, no. 38. San Francisco: Jossey-Bass, Summer 1987.

Unfortunately, minority groups have yet to realize fully the benefits of our current "land of opportunity." Those benefits, as defined by enrollment at predominantly white institutions, have eluded most minorities, despite their intellectual, cultural, and scientific contributions to the development and advancement of this nation.

Predominantly white institutions of higher learning have underenrolled ethnic minorities, especially blacks, Hispanic groups, and American Indians, while Asian American students are channelled disproportionately into technical/scientific disciplines and underrepresented in the social and behavioral sciences (Astin, 1982; Suzuki, 1983). Failure to educate ethnic minority citizens properly affects the entire nation adversely. One has only to consider the contributions of such Americans as the astronaut Guy Bluford or former Congresswoman Barbara Jordan to realize the array of talent available in the minority population, a pool of talent that is wasted if ignored. Unless America's colleges and universities can educate ethnic minority students for intellectual and political leadership roles in the twenty-first century, this nation may be labeled the land of lost opportunity.

Early Minority Student Involvement

The history of U.S. minorities is intertwined with the growth of American colleges. Unfortunately, during most of this history, the relationship between minority students and predominantly white institutions was an adversarial one. White institutions did not support minority students' efforts to matriculate.

During those early days, minority students attended selected colleges, and only under carefully controlled conditions. Black participation in higher education, for example, was "imperceptible" until the Civil War (Weinberg, 1977b, p. 6). By approximately 1865, American universities nationwide had graduated only between fifteen and twenty-eight blacks. Before 1865, Southern universities and colleges totally excluded blacks; not until after World War I were blacks permitted to attend any public white colleges in the South.

Of course, racism was not limited to Southern colleges. Northern colleges did not embrace black students readily. Even among such foremost Northern universities as Columbia, Harvard, and the University of Chicago, black student enrollment and campus living arrangements were restricted significantly. At the University of Dayton, blacks were officially excluded from day classes, in deference to Southern white students, and Skidmore College accepted blacks only as day students. Blacks were required to maintain separate residences and dining facilities at many colleges. In 1931, institutions excluding blacks from college dormitories included the state universities of Iowa, Arizona, and Michigan as well as the private schools Bryn Mawr, Macalester, Temple, and Villanova (Weinberg, 1977b).

Blacks were not the only ethnic minority group whose collegiate education was restricted. During the nineteenth century, Indians were rarely enrolled in American colleges. Only in very recent history have white institutions, with any fervor, sought Indian students. Dartmouth College included in its original statement of purpose ". . . the education and Christianizing of Indians, Whites, and others . . ." (Weinberg, 1977a, p. 337). Despite this stated goal, Dartmouth graduated only 187 Indians from 1769 to 1973, an average of only one every eight years!

The collegiate history of Hispanics had scarcely begun before World War II. Even when they were admitted, Hispanics often had to deny or restrict their cultural identity in order to matriculate. Not until 1968, when reliable data on Hispanics were kept and the civil rights "La Raza" movement began, were Hispanics enrolled in any significant numbers in colleges and universities (Lopez, Madrid-Barela, and Macías, 1976). Even then, their enrollment was confined largely to two-year colleges. Today, Hispanics are still represented in colleges and universities disproportionately to the general population, even in urban Southwestern settings, where many Mexican-American Hispanics live (see Chapter Four, this volume).

As one may conclude from these examples, the United States did not embrace minority student college education with any perceptible enthusiasm. If by chance a minority student was permitted to enroll in a college, it was often in a segregated learning environment under markedly inferior conditions.

In 1954 the *Brown* v. *Board of Education of Topeka* Supreme Court decision overturned separate educational systems for blacks and (theoretically) other minorities. Only since then have predominantly white universities begun to attend actively to the education of ethnic minorities, complying only after state and federal courts ordered colleges to integrate. As late as 1986, however, a few predominantly white institutions had yet to comply fully with the 1954 mandate.

Thus, while American ethnic minorities have been involved in many aspects of American society, they have been discouraged from seeking access to higher education. Even when mandated to do so, institutions have failed to show concern for minority students. Minority students who sought the education to which they were entitled attended college under hostile environmental conditions, and often under physical and psychological duress.

Despite overwhelming odds, however, ethnic minorities have enrolled in predominantly white colleges and universities, and a select few have been graduated from them. When we consider these enrollment and graduation successes, it is important for us to realize the multitude of social and environmental factors that have affected minorities' involvement with American colleges and universities.

8

Factors Influencing Minority Enrollment

Several social, political, and economic factors have influenced institutions to admit minority students. These factors include the civil rights movement; changes in federal support to higher education; immigration patterns and related legislation; statehood; and World War II and other conflicts.

Civil Rights Movement. Perhaps no other reform movement has had a more dramatic impact on the enrollment of minority students than the civil rights movement, which utilized armies of minority and white college students for its struggle and designated the college campus as its battleground. The civil rights movement sought minority student matriculation, using legislated mandates and, in some cases, the National Guard and federal troops' support to ensure minority students' access to and entrance into white institutions. Northern and Southern colleges alike became battlefields, but especially the Southern schools, including universities in Arkansas, Texas, Oklahoma, Virginia, Alabama, Mississippi, and Georgia. The civil rights era witnessed massive enrollment of ethnic minorities in colleges. This increase was due in large part to efforts toward basic educational entitlements through legislation, court orders, voting, and—in some unfortunate instances—violence.

Federal Support for Higher Education. During the 1960s, the federal government, especially under the Kennedy and Johnson administrations, created education and training programs for the educationally and economically "disadvantaged." Programs ranging from the Job Corps to Head Start began and provided basic education skills to thousands of undereducated minority participants. Simultaneously, because of increased pressure to train more scientists for the space program, the federal government made new financial resources available to higher education for basic research, training, and individual student support. Collectively, these two influences contributed to increases in financial aid for college to groups of previously underenrolled students. Programs such as the Pell Grants, the National Defense and National Direct Student Loans, and College Work-Study were instituted. The availability of such funding for colleges, coupled with federal financial support for the "disadvantaged," meant significant numbers of working-class persons, including some belonging to ethnic minorities, entered colleges for the first time.

Changes in Immigration Patterns. Since the turn of the century and beyond, the United States has witnessed major immigrations of Chinese, Cuban, Filipino, Indochinese, Japanese, Korean, Mexican, and Vietnamese people into this country. Causes include war or other military engagements, postwar reparations, economic disaster, and the Communist takeover of such countries as Cuba, Vietnam, Cambodia, and Korea. As a result of economic hardship, the United States has also experienced an influx of immigrants from our southern neighbor, Mexico. Over the years, the United States has resettled many ethnic minorities who, having obtained citizenship, became eligible for college education. The immigration rates of these minorities were restricted by carefully planned guidelines. Among those immigration enactments were (1) the Chinese Exclusion Act of 1882, which excluded Chinese and was not repealed until World War II; (2) the Immigration Exclusion Act of 1924, which dramatically restricted immigration of many Asians; (3) *Ozawa* versus *U.S.* (November 13, 1932), which deemed Japanese immigrants "ineligible for citizenship"; and (4) the Immigration Act of 1965 (Chan and Tsang, 1983; Suzuki, 1983; Yoshiwara, 1983; Macaranas, 1983). The most recent immigration legislation—the 1986 Immigration Reform Act—grants amnesty to undocumented workers who have resided in the United States since 1982 and imposes legal sanctions on individuals who hire undocumented workers.

Just as political and socioeconomic influences restricted the entry of many ethnic groups into the United States, so were minorities also later restricted from access to higher education. Such changes in immigration practice both stem from and evoke changes in a nation's perceptions of particular ethnic groups.

Statehood. Since the early 1900s, five former U.S territories have become states—Arizona, Oklahoma, New Mexico, Alaska, and Hawaii—and one commonwealth, Puerto Rico, has been created. Land acquisitions have increased the numbers of U.S. minorities available for and entitled to college education. These groups include Aleuts; Chinese; Eskimos; Filipinos; Guamanians; several Indian tribes, pueblos, or nations; Japanese; native Hawaiians; Mexican Americans; Puerto Ricans; and Samoans. Regardless of their sources, additions to the ethnic plurality of this nation increase the challenge for our institutions of higher education to meet their responsibilities to educate citizens. As new citizens claim the rights of their citizenship, colleges and universities must prepare to provide them education.

World War II and Other Conflicts. Few would deny that World War II—as well as other, undeclared conflicts, such as the Korean and Vietnamese wars—left indelible marks on the United States. These conflicts have affected U.S. ethnic minorities in unfortunate ways, evidenced today by long-held prejudices and biases, which originated during wartime.

World War II brought the internment of thousands of Japanese citizens under Executive Order 9066, which authorized the removal of "all persons of Japanese ancestry from the West Coast" and spawned over four hundred anti-Japanese laws (Yoshiwara, 1983, p. 18). Such government actions restricted enrollment in or graduation from several colleges and cost Japanese American families millions of dollars in lost education. To date, the United States has yet to make full reparation to Japanese Americans for the loss of all their civil rights; litigation continues for redress and reparation.

The Japanese Americans were not the only minorities affected by World War II. On the West Coast, Chinese Americans faced discrimination during the same time, when biased, misinformed non-Asians mistook them for Japanese and consequently included them in their mistreatment of Japanese Americans. Black soldiers, fighting in segregated military units throughout most of America's wars, faced both enemy troops and racism. They returned from more recent wars to find that segregated colleges still denied them admission, despite their GI Bill financing.

The net effect of wars on the college education of minorities was mixed. A small number of minority persons, most of them men who had known combat leadership and battle honors, benefited from veterans' programs and attended predominantly white institutions. An even smaller percentage of that elite group actually graduated. The bulk of America's ethnic minorities—despite their having purchased war bonds, complied with gasoline rationing, worked in ammunition plants and shipyards, and fought in the war—"celebrated" victory in still-segregated communities and colleges.

As a result of this series of historical events, then, U.S. minorities received mixed support for entrance into predominantly white colleges and universities. The overall effect of these and other historical events is not known, since they continue to create history, pressing on minorities the necessity for college education and pressing on campuses the need to redefine themselves in order to accommodate the students of the future— minorities. To redefine their missions and to assist minority students through this redefinition, colleges must understand just how minority students develop and grow as they seek college education.

Limitation of Student Development Models

Minority college student development has been virtually ignored in the college literature. While the 1960s and the 1970s brought voluminous research on minority students, that research was concerned largely with comparing minorities to white students on several psychological and social dimensions. Rarely did investigators concern themselves with defining factors that promoted minority students' overall intellectual and psychological development. This early research and its theoretical underpinnings fell short in several ways. Of the various theories or models of college student development, few clearly characterized the culture-specific aspects of development. Most theories presumed that all students experienced developmental phenomena similarly. Only rarely did those theories discuss cultural factors, except in cross-race developmental research conceptualized only to validate existing theory. Current theories or models of college student development also fail to account for the influence of culture on the developmental process; they lack sufficient understanding of minority students.

To understand minority students' development thoroughly rec an examination of social environmental factors, such as economics (especially poverty), ethnic or cultural background, and racial and gender bias and their interactive effects on American society and on minority college students' growth. Current student developmental theories fail to understand these phenomena, yet these environmental factors influence ethnic minorities in significant and often adverse ways. Student affairs practitioners charged with facilitating minority students' development in college need to understand and weigh all such social environmental factors.

Most current student developmental theories presume that growth occurs within a monolingual, supportive living/learning environment. Yet many American ethnic minorities, especially in the American Indian, Hispanic, and Asian American subcultures, live and learn in bilingual/bicultural environments, settings with languages, customs, and value systems that differ from and often conflict with those found at college. Moreover, the assumption of a supportive environment ignores the unhappy fact that minorities are expected consistently to learn and develop within hostile environments—poor, austere, racially biased, and economically deprived settings that hinder rather than support students' development. These theories fail to articulate how students' development is either stifled or facilitated by students' preferences within such hostile environments.

Few developmental theories recognize the role of assimilation/acculturation in a students' overall developmental process. While there have been a few researchers, such as Cross (1971), who have posited acculturation/assimilation models, these models have been neither accepted nor embraced readily by mainstream theorists. The reluctance of mainstream theorists to understand assimilation or acculturation variables may produce a conflict for one who tries to apply mainstream theory to minority students. Since they take no account of acculturation, traditional theorists overlook an important dimension of minority students' development: adjusting to living/learning in a campus environment that varies from the accustomed cultural frame of reference. Minority students' college experiences are distinguished from those of white students along the dimension of acculturation. Most white students do not experience acculturation, at least not to the degree that minority students do.

A final limitation concerns current developmental theories' emphasis on Euro-Western values. Colleges and universities in the United States adhere to these values; their influence is seen in the ideals that guide our educational processes and in educators' approaches to college students. Euro-Western values include emphasis on individualism and individual achievement, long-range goals, mastery over one's environment, cause-effect relationships, competition, and structured time orientation. In sharp constrast, American ethnic minority groups hold ideals and values that in practice may be quite different from Euro-Western values. Minority values may include emphasis on family or collective group, restraint of feelings, private expression of emotions, present or flexible time orientation, preservation of the past, living harmoniously with one's environment, and cooperation. Most current developmental theories have been elaborated by nonminority persons, who are likely to adhere to more traditional Euro-Western values than to those espoused by minority group members. As such, the value orientations (especially those stressing individual achievement and competition) of current theory do not recognize and understand minority values.

Thus, while mainstream student development theories appear sound and logical and are based in empirical evidence, they have shortcomings. These shortcomings do not undercut the legitimacy of these theories, but they do warrant the observation that cultural aspects of growth and development are not explained sufficiently by mainstream theories.

Professionals who employ student development theories, either in their research or in service delivery to minority students, should make efforts to understand cultural and social environmental variables as they relate to specific minority group members. Consultation with minority student affairs professionals or with minority behavioral science academicians may be useful for clarifying the insufficiently explained factors that affect minority students on college campuses. Training can show staff how to help professionals apply mainstream theories in new and innovative ways to minority student development. The need for this kind of understanding is obvious; effective programs and services for minority students cannot be successfully implemented without it. Therefore, student affairs professionals must admit their own naiveté, as a crucial step toward increasing their knowledge.

Student Development Theory and Minority Students

Before one can conduct successful services and programs for ethnic minority students, one must understand how minority students develop as they pursue college education. Understanding minority students' development on predominantly white campuses is especially critical, since their development must continue in settings quite different from their home environments. Minority student development, while believed to follow patterns of growth similar to those of other college students, also reflects cultural and ethnic differences in progression through developmental stages.

Stikes (1984) observed that minority student development appeared to follow the basic pattern of student development "except for the peculiarities associated with race and culture . . . the definition of race carries with it certain positive/negative consequences that affect student development in American colleges and universities" (p. 87). Minority student development should be understood thoroughly if practitioners are to succeed in their education efforts to retain minorities. Among the developmental issues for minority students are the following.

Academic and Intellectual Competence. Often, minority students arrive on campus academically underprepared and may not have achieved fully within their learning environments, for several reasons: poorly equipped schools; interference of student discipline problems with learning; peer pressure that does not support development of intellectual competencies or gives conflicting messages; interference with the learning process from racial insensitivity, poverty, and other social factors; and lack of learning and reinforcement of perseverance, motivation, delayed gratification, tolerance for ambiguity, and other psychological correlates of mastery.

The composite effect of these and other factors contributes to the fact that many minority students arrive on college campuses less than well prepared to tackle college curricula. At a time in our educational history when 30 to 40 percent of entering students lack the basic skills necessary to college-level performance, this underpreparedness is not limited to minority students; yet they, far more frequently than others, suffer the stigma and often receive the least support for enhancing their skills (Moore and Carpenter, 1985). Minority and other underprepared students should be assisted to change and enhance their academic and intellectual skills to their fullest potential.

Establishing and Maintaining Interpersonal Relationships. Healthy, intimate relationships with the same- and opposite-sex peers is an area laden with cultural and value differences. Added to the usual adolescent issues are the realities of being "the only minority" in the residence hall, the classroom, or the organization. Relationships for minority students are complicated further by the small number of minority peers. This relative isolation can contribute to feelings of loneliness and alienation (Fleming, 1981). These feelings, coupled with the pressures associated with "forced" interaction with minority peers simply because "we are the only ones," often contribute to an artificially contrived environment that precludes healthy relationships. Further complicating healthy relationships for minorities are biases of race, gender, and social class. Such biases undercut the minority students' ability to trust peers and devalue the minority student, thereby encouraging imbalanced relationships. A perceived disproportionate minority male/female ratio, plus the self- or socially imposed double standards regarding interracial dating, add even further complications. These factors and others can grievously restrict minority students' relationships at college. Student affairs professionals must understand and consider such moderating factors if they are to promote the developmental growth of the minority student.

Developing Healthy Sex Roles and Sexual Identity. Important to the development of autonomy and self-identity is an understanding of oneself as an adult man or woman. Unfortunately, colleges in general are ineffective in helping minority students develop proper sex roles. Development as a black man or a Chicana or a Filipino male on white campuses often involves cultural and racial biases, misinformation, and stereotypes, all of which devalue the individual, thereby lowering self-esteem. Development may best be achieved through role modeling and peer support activities to help confirm minority students' progress through these dimensions. Activities such as the University of Texas at Austin Counseling and Mental Health Center's support groups for black men and women and Hispanic men and women help in attaining this goal.

Developing Career/Life-Style Plans. Often minority students arrive on campus with naive perceptions regarding their life plans and future careers. Many students feel pressure to decide upon a curriculum because later it will lead to high salaries and will provide enough income to send money home to the family.

Minority students, more than most, require exposure to a variety of career and vocational options. They should be challenged to make choices that integrate vocational interests with cultural background and academic skill potential. Minority students should also be taught that their bilingualism is a valuable skill to be highlighted and marketed, rather than denied or ignored.

Maintaining Personal Health and Wellness. Among the issues of importance to minority college students is developing a healthy life-style while recognizing the relationship between one's personal health and wellness and academic excellence and achievement. Often, because of economic and social factors, including poverty and inadequate health care in childhood, minority students enter college not understanding that good health is an asset to success in college.

In addition, minorities, especially blacks, may have increased risk of developing certain chronic and potential life-threatening health problems because of dietary habits, predisposition factors, poor exposure to medical resources, and living with a chronic basal level of stress (Myers, 1982). Heart disease, alcoholism, hypertension, and other potentially chronic problems can be managed early if students learn healthy life-style habits through appropriate education and exposure to preventive, healthful activities. The college experience presents an excellent opportunity for students to reevaluate health-risk factors and, if necessary, develop sounder attitudes and behaviors.

Campus mental and general health resources should encourage minority students to participate regularly in their programs and services. For example, minority students should be advised to have regular health examinations and to use such preventive measures such as stress, weight, and behavioral management programs; gynecological exams; contraception; smoking-cessation workshops, nutrition workshops, and exercise programs.

The goal of such programs is for minority students to learn that maintaining positive physical and mental health is essential to academic success.

Key to minorities' participation in campus health and wellness activities is the visible participation of minority staff, faculty, and peers in all health programs as a way of giving students emotional support for making health changes. Health and counseling centers should make every effort to promote role models by hiring minority staff for campus health services as well as in the academic and student affairs areas.

Formulating an Integrated Philosophy of Life. Minority students, like other collegiates, need assistance in establishing and affirming life values and learning how those values govern their decisions and life plans. As they struggle with adopting personal values, minority students may raise culture-specific questions: How can I retain my cultural values and attend a white institution? How can I repay my family for allowing me to be the first to attend college? Must I return to the reservation and work there once I complete my education? How can the university support me and care about minorities if it does not support divestiture from South African interests? Is that attitude racist? Is it wrong not to like whites? Minority students' concerns regarding philosophical beliefs and values are often tied to questions about cultural identity.

Participation in and guidance of students' development of value systems is one of the most awesome of higher education's responsibilities. To achieve this monumental task for all students, institutions must not indiscriminately impose their Anglo and often middle-class values. Rather, they must create environments that permit students to develop and affirm their specific cultural values while learning to appreciate the differing yet positive values of others.

Religion remains an important activity for minority students during the college years. Through student activities and informal programs, colleges can support students as they affirm and enhance their religious beliefs. Students should be encouraged to establish such groups as the Korean Christian Students Association, the Black Christians Group, the Buddhist Association and to stage such events as the University of Texas at Austin's 1986 Gospel Fest or its Inner Visions of Blackness Gospel Choir.

Developing Cultural Esthetics and Awareness. Colleges should provide frameworks in which students can develop appreciation for their own cultures while recognizing the beauty of other cultures. Programs such as Cinco de Mayo, Black History Month, Chinese New Year, Indian Pow Wow, and Martin Luther King, Jr., Day are excellent avenues for promoting cultural awareness. In addition, campus art galleries should make every effort to display and promote the art of minority and Third World artists and cultures. Even the campus carillons can add to awareness if *Lift Every Voice and Sing* (the black national anthem) or other ethnic songs are played.

Developing Social Responsibility. Minority students, because of their ethnicity status and exposure to the real and perceived social injustices of racism, sexism, and poverty, enter college with a strong sense of social responsibility. Many are the children of activists in the civil rights movement and bring with them a keen social responsibility for righting some historical educational injustices. It is not surprising that minority students assume leadership for such campus advocacy activities as agitating for divestiture or promoting increased minority student services programs.

The dilemma for minority students is seldom whether to accept social responsibility; for them, that question is answered by virtue of their minority status in a white world. For minority students, the dilemma is more often how to balance their social responsibilities with their commitment to educational objectives. All too often, minority students overinvolve themselves in social advocacy, to the detriment of their academic work. Student affairs practitioners can help minority students realize that performing well academically is integral to the development of social responsibility by emphasizing and explaining how technicians, scientists, medical personnel, philosophers, educators, lawyers, and social scientists are essential to correcting injustices and to ensuring basic entitlements. Minority students who are challenged to view academic achievement as a social responsibility and who learn to balance their studying with advocacy activities are the ones who graduate and participate in community and world affairs responsibly.

The Campus Environment and Minority Students

A racially naive or insensitive campus environment, one that is nonaccepting of minority students' cultural and racial distinctiveness, can thwart or stifle development. In turn, thwarted development places students at risk educationally and emotionally.

In a classic study of black students' development on predominantly white campuses, Fleming (1984) found that covert and overt racism in faculty-student relations creates a climate of hostility and rejection for some blacks and other minorities. A campus climate of racism is not conducive to optimal academic performance; it can restrict the fulfillment of the primary psychological needs of late adolescence.

Minority college students placed in an environment that fails to acknowledge or recognize them fully may experience social isolation, loneliness, and alienation. These outcomes adversely affect academic success. Such environments impede minority students' movement toward mastering increasingly complex tasks, thereby restricting their development.

What happens when minority students remain in unsupportive campus environments? For some, staying creates internal dissonance and conflict. There is an optimum level of disequilibrium or dissonance requisite to growth; but beyond that level, counterproductive tension, psychological distress, and anxiety occur. Over time, these psychological problems may lead to severe anxiety, depression, psychosomatic illness, or major psychiatric disturbance. An unsupportive campus environment contributes to a student's lowered satisfaction with college and can result in a premature exit from campus without a degree. This is society's loss, a loss that can be prevented if colleges and universities design effective programs to promote minority student development.

Strategies for Promoting Minority Student Development

How can institutions change their campus climates to promote minority student development? Implementing high-quality programs and services for minority students requires multiple modes of intervention and the use of a variety of change-oriented options. Often minority students are required to learn and develop in two cultures, and sometimes those cultures espouse conflicting or even diametrically opposed values. Multiple intervention modes are essential to working with such cultural diversity.

Changing the Institution–Minority Student Relationship. Acceptance of the unpleasant reality regarding the relationship between white institutions and minority students precedes creation of effective programs. Until quite recently, the relationship between predominantly white institutions and minority students, especially blacks and Hispanics, has been an inequitable one; it has been one-directional. Institutions have sought to direct minority students' educational experiences, arguing that they had much to offer them. The assumption of institutions is that the minority student has little or nothing to offer in return, except a body for the "affirmative action, end-of-year statistics." Rarely have predominantly white institutions believed that their settings would be enhanced by the enrollment of ethnic minority students.

This patronizing, we-know-best attitude has contributed in turn to a misconception among minority groups: "If my group is noticed by the administration, we must be a 'special' group. The white administration will now protect me because I am special." This competitive stance, this vying for patronization and protection based on some fleeting and unpredictable sense of "specialness" (this year we feature Asians; save Hispanics for an election year) fosters interethnic group conflicts, which are detrimental to development among minority students of all origins. This stance also does a disservice to confused and well-meaning but ignorant white students. Moreover, this attitude reinforces minority groups' dependence on white college administrations for their group identity. Within such patronizing climates, other biases, racism, sexism, and elitism flourish. On such campuses, few students, white or minority, can develop. Without the development of its young, a nation has no future.

Improving Retention of Minority Students. College efforts to recruit, enroll, and retain students has been operationally defined as an institutional rather than individual developmental task. If one asks a college administrator for a definition, one may hear *retention* described as some numerically based process of retaining and recording the number of chosen minorities on any campus in any given year. Retention, to the institution, becomes a work function or task; it represents the campus "hit rate" of the number of successful minority students out of the total recruited.

Rarely is retention conceptualized as a student development task, nor is it perceived as an individual process; yet if institutions are committed to having these college students succeed, then retention must be reframed as a developmental task that relies on that specific accomplishment as a basis for change. Retention, as a student developmental task, would assume the achievement and development of competence, autonomy, identity, and other developmental tasks as necessary components.

Institutions whose minority "retention" programs set as their goal the students' mastery of developmental tasks, rather than a simple counting of student enrollments or a recording of grades, will have stronger programs than campuses that do not define retention developmentally. Quite simply, institutions that are successful in retaining minority students facilitate minority students' academic, social, and personal development.

Encouraging Mentoring Relationships. While several campuses have had minority mentoring programs for some time, many programs assumed one-directional mentoring relationships: The faculty or staff member gave his or her expertise, time, and wisdom to the younger minority student, who was merely the beneficiary of the process. This model is an inefficient one and neglects the two-way nature of true mentoring. By this omission, the minority student is deprived of potential learning from the mentor.

Mentoring relationships in their purest form are two-way relationships, with faculty member and student both benefiting. The key to successful mentoring, however, is to ensure that both parties grow personally from the interaction. Ideally, mentoring will best facilitate a minority student's development when the faculty or staff person's own needs are met, especially if such interactions facilitate mastery of generativity.

Integral to the mastery of generativity is concern for future generations, an altruistic concern for others, and a desire to pass values on to a new generation. The mastery of generativity, for minority and white faculty and staff, helps to create a climate in which minority students can achieve autonomy and responsibility for self, ethnic self-identity, and other age-appropriate developmental tasks.

In short, mentoring programs provide opportunities for faculty and staff to develop so that they may then return energies and expertise to minority students by their care and genuine interest in their welfare. Minority student development is particularly enhanced by interaction with older minority faculty and staff persons. Campuswide minority mentoring projects that enhance personal growth both for faculty and for students simultaneously take the leadership in promoting minority student development.

Encouraging Intentional Student Development Activities. Minority student organizations offer a myriad activities that intentionally promote students' development within a cultural framework, yet student affairs professionals are often too naive or insensitive to recognize this resource. Take, for example, the many activities urging divestiture from South Africa. Such campus activism is an excellent framework for intentional student development, as it represents challenges that closely resemble realities students will encounter once they leave campus. Guiding students to articulate their rationales for divestiture exposes students to moral dilemmas; the resolution of such real-life dilemmas promotes and complements more traditional methods of moral development.

In addition, persuading students to speak at a noon divestiture rally helps minority students adopt new thinking strategies while altering beliefs and enhancing their own development of basic self-identity, concurrently with supporting a political cause. Minority students, who may be faced with protecting a South African–style shanty from being destroyed by disgruntled opponents, learn responsibility and concern for the welfare of others as they confront new thinking about moral issues. Student affairs departments, especially campus activities and residence halls, can find an ideal "living laboratory" for personal development in the minority campus organizations if only they will accept these new avenues for promoting student development. Minority (and nonminority) campus organizations provide extraordinary outlets for the promotion of minority student development.

Changing the Campus Climate. Minority student development cannot occur on campuses that students perceive as hostile and unsupportive. These settings tolerate racism, sexism, and other overt and covert biases. Perhaps the most important ingredient of promoting minority student development is a healthy, bias-free campus environment. Institutions that minorities perceive as negative and hostile have already undermined and doomed all their efforts to support and "retain" minority students. They give minority students a mixed message: "I'm really not sure I want you here, but I needed to recruit you."

Too many minority students perceive too many college campuses as hostile, according to Astin (1982), Fleming (1981, 1984), and others. Minority students are too often placed in psychological jeopardy. Institutions that desire to see minority (and all other) students develop fully must eradicate all biases on their campuses: in classroom instruction, electronic media, printed material, attitude, or behavior. This feat is no small task. Nevertheless, a total commitment to this task must become an institutional mission, mandated by the president or provost, the board of regents or trustees, and the chief student affairs officer, to be fulfilled by all faculty, staff, administrators, and students. Any compromise jeopardizes the continued development of minority students and all others on the college campus. Institutions must eradicate climates hostile to student development if they intend to survive and flourish in the next decade.

Conclusion

College archives reveal that minorities have sought matriculation into colleges and universities for several decades, yet only in the last two have they realized their desire in significant numbers. Today, as higher education sheds its old perceptions and beliefs about ethnic minorities, it enters a new era. Colleges and universities, if they intend to mature, must respond to minority students' developmental needs and must meet those needs successfully. Assisting minority students to develop academically, socially, and personally helps colleges ensure their futures by educating competent young men and women to act responsibly in the world. Certainly, those beginnings for minority students promise enduring growth for higher education, and everyone will benefit.

References

Astin, A. *Minorities in American Higher Education: Recent Trends, Current Prospects, and Recommendations.* San Francisco: Jossey-Bass, 1982.

Chan, K. S., and Tsang, S. "Overview of the Educational Process of Chinese Americans." In D. T. Nakanishi and M. Hirano-Nakanishi (eds.), *The Education of Asian and Pacific Americans: Historical Perspectives and Prescriptions for the Future.* Phoenix, Ariz.: Oryx Press, 1983.

Cross, W. E. "The Thomas and Cross Models of Psychological Nigrescense: A Review." *Journal of Black Psychology,* 1971, 5, 13–31.

Fleming, J. "Special Needs of Blacks and Other Minorities." In A. Chickering (ed.), *The Modern American College: Responding to the New Realities of Diverse Students and a Changing Society.* San Francisco: Jossey-Bass, 1981.

Fleming, J. *Blacks in College: A Comparative Study of Students' Success in Black and in White Institutions.* San Francisco: Jossey-Bass, 1984.

Lopez, R. W., Madrid-Barela, A., and Macías, R. F. *Chicanos in Higher Education.* Monograph no. 7. Los Angeles: Chicano Studies Center Publication, University of California, 1976.

Macaranas, F. M. "Socioeconomic Issues Affecting the Education of Minority Groups: The Case of Filipino Americans." In D. T. Nakanishi and M. Hirano-Nakanishi (eds.), *The Education of Asian and Pacific Americans: Historical Perspectives and Prescriptions for the Future.* Phoenix, Ariz.: Oryx Press, 1983.

Moore, W., and Carpenter, L. C. "Academically Underprepared Students." In L. Noel, R. Levitz, D. Saluri, and Associates (eds.), *Increasing Student Retention: Effective Programs and Practices for Reducing the Dropout Rate.* San Francisco: Jossey-Bass, 1985.

Myers, H. "Stress, Ethnicity, and Social Class: A Model for Research with Black

21

Populations." In E. Jones and S. Korchin (eds.), *Minority Mental Health*. New York: Praeger, 1982.

Stikes, C. S. *Black Students in Higher Education*. Carbondale: Southern Illinois University Press, 1984.

Suzuki, B. H. "The Education of Asian and Pacific Americans: An Introductory Overview." In D. T. Nakanishi and M. Hirano-Nakanishi (eds.), *The Education of Asian and Pacific Americans: Historical Perspectives and Prescriptions for the Future*. Phoenix, Ariz.: Oryx Press, 1983.

Weinberg, M. A. *A Chance to Learn: The History of Race and Education in the U.S.* London: Cambridge University Press, 1977a.

Weinberg, M. *Minority Students: A Research Appraisal*. Washington, D.C.: U.S. Department of Health, Education, and Welfare, National Institute of Education, 1977b.

Yoshiwara, F. M. "Shattering Myths: Japanese-American Education Issues." In D. T. Nakanishi and M. Hirano-Nakanishi (eds.), *The Education of Asian and Pacific Americans: Historical Perspectives and Prescriptions for the Future*. Phoenix, Ariz.: Oryx Press, 1983.

Doris J. Wright is a staff psychologist at the Counseling and Mental Health Center at the University of Texas at Austin. Since 1970, she has worked with minority students on six campuses. She writes frequently on minority student development.

Black students' needs have changed from those of their predecessors. These changes lead practitioners to reexamine how they provide student services to them.

Black Students' Needs on Predominantly White Campuses

Augustine W. Pounds

Black students have pursued matriculation into America's colleges and universities for over 125 years. Frequently, the protection and enforcement of the right to a college education has required National Guard intervention and federal mandates. Despite the opposition of public officials, particularly in the South, to their enrollment, blacks have managed to enroll in and graduate from American colleges and universities in increasing numbers until quite recently. Even as the struggle to admit, retain, and ultimately graduate black collegians continues today, colleges face new challenges from this vocal black student constituency to create optimal learning environments that promote retention to graduation of America's high-tech black youth.

This chapter deals with these challenges and describes how black students experience college today. In addition, program strategies are outlined to help student affairs practitioners respond more completely to black college students' academic, social, and emotional needs. The first step toward understanding and responding to those needs is recognition of the road blacks have traveled seeking matriculation into American colleges and universities.

D. J. Wright (ed.). *Responding to the Needs of Today's Minority Students.*
New Directions for Student Services, no. 38. San Francisco: Jossey-Bass, Summer 1987.

Historical Overview

Educational attainment has been a long-held value within black communities; unfortunately, American colleges and universities did not noticeably support this value until just prior to the Civil War. For most of America's first one hundred years, its black citizens were denied access to most colleges and universities. As will be seen, the history of black progress in higher education until the Sixties has been characterized by monumental efforts on the part of blacks and by relentless resistance and indifference from the larger society (Morris, 1979).

Blacks were excluded from public and private universities almost entirely in America's early history. The growth of black enrollment in institutions of higher education occurred with the establishment of the historically and/or traditionally black colleges of the South. Wilberforce College, Morehouse College, Lincoln, Shaw, and Howard universities were established in the 1850s as part of this program of self-education (Fleming, 1984). Black efforts were extended by Northern missionaries, resulting in the creation of black colleges, Fisk University and Talledega College, in 1865 by the American Missionary Association. The Reconstruction Era, 1868–1877, witnessed an explosion of higher educational opportunities for blacks. While Northern freed blacks and concerned white Northern missionaries advocated a liberal arts education for blacks, Southern educators and politicians believed that blacks were intellectually inferior and were entitled only to a separate education of lower caliber, a position readily adopted by others throughout the South. As a result, separate development of segregated black schools began and received federal support when the Supreme Court upheld the doctrine of "separate but equal" in *Plessy* v. *Ferguson* (Bullock, cited in Fleming, 1984, p. 12).

During the post-Reconstruction period and into the 1890s, forty private and seventeen public black colleges were created, reinforcing the Southern "separate but equal" doctrine. These early black colleges offered predominantly primary and secondary education; only later did several evolve into normal schools offering college programs. While these colleges contributed significantly to a reduction of black illiteracy, white Southern public officials viewed such institutions as providing a lower quality of education; consequently, so Southern logic argued, they should receive fewer educational resources than their white counterparts. This twisted, distorted logic was believed to have influenced the passage of the Second Morrill Act of 1890, which authorized the creation of black land-grant colleges, where states maintained segregated education. These colleges contained inferior facilities and poorly prepared teachers, in contrast to the Southern white land-grant schools, where adequate resources and well-trained faculty obtained. None of these seventeen black land-grant colleges offered a liberal arts education before 1916 (Fleming, 1984).

By 1930, black colleges enrolled approximately 19,000 students, and black colleges began to educate more students, as increasing numbers of blacks sought further training in white colleges (Aptheker, cited in Fleming, 1981). A handful of black graduates sought advanced degrees at white institutions; it is estimated that 119 blacks received degrees from white institutions, including the noted black educator W.E.B. Du Bois (Fleming, 1984).

Of course, because not all blacks were readily accepted into white colleges, many legal challenges to their educational entitlements occurred. The first of many legal challenges to enrollment in white colleges and universities began as early as 1935, when Donald Murry sued the University of Maryland when he was denied admission to its law school. This suit was followed by four other lawsuits: *Missouri ex rel Gaines* v. *Canada* (1938), *Sipuel* v. *Board of Regents* (1948), *Sweatt* v. *Painter* (1950), and *McLaurin* v. *Oklahoma State Board of Regents* (1950) (Fleming, 1984). Collectively, they paved the way for the historic 1954 *Brown* v. *Board of Education of Topeka*, which ordered the desegregation of school systems. As a result of the Brown and other court cases, higher education was forced to redefine the way it enrolled college students. Overall impact on American colleges and universities has been dramatic and far-reaching. The 1954 *Brown* decision was clarified later, in the 1973 *Adams* v. *Richardson* case, by the ruling that states had to rid themselves of their dual systems of higher education for blacks and whites (Fleming, 1984).

The South was not the only place where black students sought entry into colleges. Black college students were not present in large numbers in the North until prior to World War II (Mingle, 1981). Because of the black migration to the North and return of black GIs from World War II, black enrollment accelerated during the late Forties and early Fifties. It has been estimated that black enrollment in white colleges outside the South in 1947 was 61,000, or 3 percent of the total enrollment for white colleges. That year, black enrollment nationwide represented 6 percent, a high not reached again until 1967 (Arce, cited in Mingle, 1981).

During the late Sixties, black enrollment enjoyed a dramatic surge, topping out at 8.4% of the entire college population in 1971 and increasing steadily until the late Seventies, when total black enrollment began to decline (Thomas, 1981).

Black collegiate education has come far in a scant 125 years. Legitimately, most blacks will argue that it has not come far enough. The success of black collegians is linked to the overall expansion of public and private support for higher education. For this reason, it is important to have a historical perspective on today's black college students, a thorough understanding of their perceptions of college, and a clear statement of those programs and services that will promote their overall growth and ultimate educational success. To understand black college students' needs, colleges must become aware of the issues that affect black access to and success in college.

Issues in Black College Student Success

Black college students experience developmental issues similar to those of other college students: adjusting to college, separating from family, developing autonomy, developing career and life plans, and realizing educational goals. Black students may experience these developmental concerns differently from other students, given the influence of social, economic, and political variables. These variables qualify the ways in which black students experience the college environment. These include social adjustments, financial aid, developmental changes, nonsegregated living/learning environments, and talent development.

Social Adjustment. Black students, like other students, desire to understand how to make friends, learn about the college environment, and make the transition away from home. These developmental concerns can present unique challenges for black students if they perceive little within their environment that allows them to experience a sense of belonging—an essential component for social adjustment. In addition, black students on white campuses with small numbers of blacks may find it difficult to find and interact with black peers, and the resultant loneliness complicates their adjustment to the campus.

Financial Aid. For black families, even middle-class ones, finding money to support a college education is a difficult and oftentimes impossible task. Historically, that financial support has come from various federal monies, with matching awards from either the respective state or the home institution. Unfortunately, black students in the next decade will not have readily available federal financial support as in years past because of massive cuts to higher education during the Nixon and Reagan administrations. Colleges and universities must realize that adequate financial support is essential if they are to succeed in graduating black students. This means that institutions need to be creative in their efforts to help black students financially through four or five years of college. Black families need to be assisted to develop "creative financing" strategies in order to help educate their children.

Promoting Developmental Growth. As noted earlier, young black students share many of the developmental challenges of most college students; unfortunately, many must meet these developmental challenges in campus environments that they perceive as unresponsive, nonsupportive, and self-negating. Cultural or racial identity is an integral part of their step toward self-identity. Campus environments often covertly promote the message that black students are not valued and welcomed; this covert message conflicts with their efforts to recruit blacks and leaves the students who do enroll with mixed perceptions of their value to the institution. Environmental perceptions can and do inhibit social, intellectual, moral, and emotional development of students. Student affairs practitioners and all faculty and staff must be exceptionally creative if they are to help black students sort out conflicting messages. A carefully prescribed balance of challenge and support is needed for black students to maximize their development during the college years.

Nonsegregated Living/Learning Environment. For some black students, enrolling in college marks the first time they have lived in or learned in an integrated environment. Despite efforts to integrate public schools, many high schools are effectively segregated because of historical housing trends, which even today remain unchanged. In settings where busing has been discontinued or was never used, as in Chicago, students continue to attend predominantly black schools. When those students arrive on college campuses, they must make several adjustments that white students do not experience. Black students must adjust to being educated with and residing with white peers. The critical issue here is one of trust, for blacks may arrive with a historical experience of mistrust or uncertainty about whites. Black students, in order to succeed on predominantly white campuses, must learn to trust their white peers, teaching faculty, and student affairs staff. White faculty and staff in turn must recognize environmental factors that inhibit development and revamp the environment to better support black students' development.

Developing Black Talent. Historically, institutions of higher learning have not understood the factors necessary to enhance the talent development of black youth. They have devoted considerable time, money, and human resources to remediating black students' academic deficiencies. While this is a worthy task, it is only one factor in the development of black college students' full potential. Black collegians bring unique learning and life skills that too often remain untapped resources, both for the institutions and for the students. What is needed are services and programs that measure the value of black students' college experiences and identify the strategies necessary to develop their unique skills. Astin (1985) was one of the first proponents of talent development as a way of educating students in American institutions. The notion has clear applicability for black students and their progression through college. Institutions are encouraged to augment existing developmental programs to include components that help black students recognize and explore their intellectual, social, cultural, and personal developmental potential.

In summary, several issues are of concern to black students and should be acknowledged and accounted for in offering services and programs to them. Certainly, black college students, like other young adults in college, face the challenges that accompany becoming an adult. They must learn to develop self-reliance, independence, and autonomy and to accept adult responsiblity. These normal challenges of young adulthood increase in complexity as black students enter unfamiliar and oftentimes unsupportive white college campuses. In addition, black students and their families have major concerns regarding financing their education, since many black parents face employment discrimination that restricts the resources available to finance college education. Perhaps the first challenges to black students upon entry to white campuses are those of learning and living within a predominantly white environment and tolerating the psychological uncertainty such an adjustment brings.

The last critical issue that influences black students is the optimum development of their intellectual talents, a task that institutions have yet to support fully. Colleges must assist black students to develop all their intellectual and social talents, so that black students can be prepared to assume future leadership roles. Certainly, as colleges enroll more diverse black student populations, new issues will emerge in the college education of black students. The aforementioned concerns are issues that student affairs practitioners must identify now, lest they lose black students. To address these issues completely requires a thorough knowledge and understanding of the black college student experience.

The Black Collegiate Experience

Two questions asked frequently by student affairs practitioners in discussing black students are "How do the black students' collegiate experiences differ from those of white college students? What impact do those differences have on student affairs programming?" As will be shown, black students' collegiate experiences differ from those of white students in several critical areas, described below.

1. *They come from diverse cultural, social, and economic backgrounds, which often are not acknowledged or appreciated on campus.* Minority students, including blacks, arrive on college campuses from diverse cultural backgrounds and represent varying social, economic, and religious statuses. They come from rural reservations, urban centers, and racially segregated or integrated communities from Alaska to Florida, and from American military installations both inside and out of the continental United States. Many maintain close ties to their extended and nuclear families and communities; some may be among the first of their families to attend college (Wright, 1984). More recently, campuses have begun to see second-generation blacks enrolling, those whose parents may have attended college in the Sixties.

2. *They come to college academically underprepared and financially disadvantaged, in part because of their attendance at understaffed, ill-equipped public schools.* Despite genuine efforts by America's public schools to upgrade public education, blacks and other minority students, and those from working-class backgrounds, matriculate from public

schools with academic skills below those of white middle-class counter-parts. Myriad reasons account for these discrepancies: poorly funded schools, disrupted learning environments due to discipline problems, erratic school attendance, and ambivalent and unsupported educational aspirations. In addition, black students often come from single-parent families, usually with a female head with even lower earning capacity than white families in similar situations. Add to this reality under- and unemployment, coupled with racism, economic discrimination, and gen-der biases, and the reasons for black college students' financial and aca-demic underpreparation become clear. Far too often, black parents simply have little or no income or savings available with which to finance a college education. In addition, they may lack the disposable income to give students extra spending money or to buy supplies and books for classes. The net effect of these factors places black, other minority, and working-class students at a disadvantage, as compared to their white counterparts.

3. *They are less satisfied and involved with campus life.* Stikes (1984) found that black students are less satisfied with college than white students because they do not participate in activities directly related to their life experiences. Student retention studies have shown that the college envi-ronment is important for predicting students' academic performance (Tinto, 1975). Maynard (1980) observed that students experienced conflict when they tried to conform to university, family, and peer group expecta-tions simultaneously. They felt overwhelmed and lost.

4. *Black students are either unaffected or negatively affected by their college environments.* Fleming (1984), in a classic study, investigated blacks at predominantly white institutions. Of the four Southern predominantly white institutions she surveyed, none was found to encourage black stu-dent growth. These colleges produced either no effect at all, gross academic deterioration, or a gain on one measure that was compromised by losses on others. Among similar schools in the North, Fleming concluded, black students were not much better off than in the Southern schools. Students at these institutions might even have been worse because "they [made] no real intellectual gains," as the school produced confusion stemming from the belief that the North, not the South, was better for blacks (p. 128).

5. *Black students feel isolated and alienated on white campuses.* The ratio of black to white students is low on many campuses, and this low visibility may contribute to students' feelings of isolation, alienation, and lack of trust. In a classic study, Willie and McCord (1972) found that black students became angry and despairing when they experienced a lack of trust. They turned to other blacks for social interaction instead of to white peers or student services. When there are few black students, other prob-lems may arise. Students tend to develop brother-sister or kinship relation-ships and view other blacks as always accessible to them. This tendency

causes discomfort for some students, who do not want to be accessible to blacks only because they are themselves black. In order to counteract feelings of alienation, institutions must help black students gain mutual trust and openness, thereby creating feelings of security and belonging (Maynard, 1980).

The point may be argued that blacks are not the only college students who experience the college campuses in the aforementioned ways. Certainly, this point is well taken; low-income whites, disabled persons, middle-class women, and other nontraditional students may experience some or all of these concerns. However, when these perceptions or experiences are framed within a climate of racial discrimination, a new picture develops, for as Stikes (1984) has noted, "racial discrimination is [the] fundamental difference between blacks and whites in society and on the college campus" (p. 103). Racial discrimination interacts with these other concerns to create a campus that is perceived and experienced by blacks differently. This fact cannot be overlooked as colleges understand the black college experience.

Practitioners should be careful not to assume that all blacks experience these environmental reactions in similar ways. Further, it should not be assumed that all black collegians are alike. Blacks on college campuses differ on social class, economic, and cultural variables. Their college experience may vary as a function of those variables and of whether they are among the first generation to attend college in their respective families.

Differences Between First- and Second-Generation College Blacks

While historically most black students arriving on college campuses were among the first persons in their families to attend college, recently colleges have begun to see the children of the Sixties black students enrolling. These latter student have parents who, because they are college-educated, have clearer expectations for their children's college experiences. These students often enter with clearer ideas of college environment norms and expectations, which means they may experience fewer adjustment and transition problems than first-generation black peers, who are blazing educational trails for their families. These intragroup differences between first- and second-generation college blacks are believed to exist, but as yet few research studies have examined this phenomenon. Nonetheless, student affairs practitioners should take note of whether a black student is the first in the family to attend college or not; this variable is important in understanding the student's transition and adjustment to college and may influence learning and developmental needs and expectations regarding college. The majority of black students who attend college today are among the first in their families to attend college; a small (but growing) number are in the latter category. Several factors contribute to the success of second-generation blacks, which may be helpful for first-generation blacks to develop; interpersonal skills appropriate to the college academic environment; an internalization and later transference of educational beliefs and values into appropriate behavioral expressions; functional peer and reference groups that are consistent with future personal, academic, and professional expectations; and an understanding of oneself as a responsible person (Scott, 1981).

Well-meaning but naive faculty and staff often treat blacks, regardless of whether they are first- or second-generation, in terms of past socialization, rather than recognizing their potential for new learning and resocialization. Faculty may remark to a black student having academic difficulty, "Oh, I really don't think you can make it in this class, why don't you drop the course?" When faculty believe in the academic potential of the students, they may say, "This course may be a challenge for you academically; however, I know you can meet the challenge successfully." The former comment may be articulated as a "failure to learn," while the latter may be construed as the student's lack of interpersonal skills or recognition, but not as a lack of the ability to learn.

A positive approach, one that affirms the student's potential for learning, incorporates two dimensions: the recognition and reconceptualization of the factors that explain the level at which each black student communicates; and the implementation of a series of corrective activities designed to develop students' interpersonal skills (Scott, 1981). Faculty and student affairs staff alike must develop a new understanding of black students, especially of first-generation blacks, before they can enhance blacks' full learning and social potential.

If colleges are to retain and graduate first-generation black students, the students themselves must learn to understand the campus political process and involve themselves in it; recognize the value of professional networks and their role in college success; strengthen their self-identity as black persons and recognize its importance for enhanced learning; and refine interpersonal skills (Scott, 1981).

Student affairs practitioners can and must play a central role in discriminating between the developmental needs of first- and second-generation black students. Once these needs are made clear, practitioners can become successful in integrating these needs into successful black student programs and services.

Historical Rationale for Black Student Services

The origins of black student support services on college campuses are not clear. Many educators speculate that black student services programs and activities evolved out of the campus "revolts" of the Sixties, during which black students demanded more culturally relevant, meaningful campus services and programs. Their evolution parallels and was a beneficiary of many of the changes made during the civil rights era.

Once colleges accepted black students onto their campuses in activities beyond athletics, they were told by assertive black students that their services did not recognize the students' different learning and cognitive styles, values, customs, and behavioral expressions, and that as a result black students' learning, social, and personal developmental needs were not being met fully. Clearly, student affairs programs and services needed revision if they intended to be responsive to black students. Several factors contributed to the development of black student services and programs: community pressure; the civil rights movement; black student activism; federal government pressure to comply with enactments or court orders reinforcing affirmative action and prohibiting discrimination in education due to race, and colleges' open-admissions policies.

Black students, like other college students, sought to find ways to become involved with campus life in ways that would promote their personal and academic growth. Unfortunately, predominantly white campuses were unprepared and ill equipped to understand and help students with social, family, economic, and cultural values different from campus norms. College campuses, if they were to properly educate these students, had to redefine their environments and shift their campus values. Such changes were not readily embraced by college educators not accustomed to educating working-class students. As a result, black students had to assert their academic, social, and political needs in order to support their own academic and personal growth. Those avenues used by blacks to support black student services are described below.

Community Pressures. Black student support services developed because of black student and community pressures for culturally relevant campus programs. Students argued that campuses were insensitive to their personal developmental needs and failed to recognize cultural differences in learning styles. Black communities protested to remove class, economic, gender, and racial biases from institutions that (they argued) prohibited blacks' open access to higher education.

Black Student Activism. Several events are believed to have influenced black student activism. As black students enrolled on college campuses, they, like other students, wanted campuses to which they could belong and in which they could grow and develop. Campuses in the Sixties and the early Seventies were perceived by blacks as lacking in cultural relevance to their experience; further, they thought campuses did not embrace their learning, social, and personal development needs. As a result, black students demonstrated on campus, demanding new courses taught by black faculty and increased student services administered by blacks and carried out by black staff. In addition, students requested black cultural activities, such as Black History Month activities, speakers, and other programs celebrating the richness of black culture. More recently, black activism has been responsible for recommending that institutions divest their South African interests.

Civil Rights Movement. The civil rights movement of the late Fifties and Sixties dramatically altered how blacks participated in American society. The movement's impact was pronounced on college campuses, where it gained steam, creating an increased political activism, "Black Pride," and heightened social awareness. National organizations such as the Student Nonviolent Coordinating Committee (SNCC), the National Association for the Advancement of Colored People (NAACP), and the Southern Christian Leadership Conference (SCLC) had armies of black college students involved in their marches, sit-ins, and other demonstrations. College campuses became a forum for the movement, for they likewise had to integrate their laboratories and classrooms.

The movement's contribution to the development of college campuses was to help ensure black students' entitlement by forcing institutions to respond to black students' needs and, in so doing, to the needs of other "disadvantaged" students. This contribution meant institutions had to revise their curricula to be relevant to black and other special populations of students, including Asian Americans, American Indians, Hispanic American groups, low-income and educationally disadvantaged whites, and middle-class women. Higher education, as a result of the civil rights movement, was forced into becoming socially and politically relevant and was accountable to its public if it failed in those endeavors.

Federal Government Pressure. With the 1954 Supreme Court ruling, *Brown* v. *Board of Education of Topeka,* colleges and universities were forced to reexamine how they enrolled students, especially black and other minority students. This ruling, coupled with federal and state legislated enactments and lower-court decisions, paved the road for blacks to acquire their entitlement to the higher education that for so many years had been denied them through one form or another of discrimination.

Colleges, in order to continue receiving federal support, had to become creative and innovative in their efforts to involve blacks in higher education. These efforts took many forms, including the creation of special programs and services especially designed to address the learning, social, financial, and personal development needs of blacks, other ethnic minorities, and the economically disadvantaged. Thus, colleges witnessed the creation of such programs as the TRIO and Upward Bound programs, which were intended by definition to assist blacks in their academic endeavors and in practice helped the poor and educationally disadvantaged of all races. Colleges themselves benefited by the addition of new staff to their campuses, some of whom were black, and by the infusion of thousands of dollars into academic coffers. Unfortunately, black student services, which began as a result of these monies, were not always absorbed or integrated into the campus mainstream; consequently, when federal monies ceased or were cut drastically during the 1970s, black student services were also cut. As a result, black student services as a formalized entity lost ground on some campuses and have yet to recover that ground.

Open Admissions. During the late Sixties and Seventies, colleges and universities were pressured by a variety of groups to open their doors to groups previously underenrolled: blacks, other ethnic minorities, middle-class women (on some campuses), and working-class individuals. As a result, several colleges changed their admissions criteria to allow "open" enrollment of a broader base of prospective students, including blacks.

Not all educators have agreed that open admissions have increased access to college. One reason is that open-admissions colleges constitute a small percentage of the available four-year colleges (Morris, 1979). In addition, because of their size, open-admissions colleges are unable to provide the same opportunities as the smaller, controlled-admissions colleges. Open-admissions institutions frequently suffer a loss of academic reputation, leading to a drain of the potentially best applicants and a decline in the value (marketability) of the degree (Castro, cited in Morris, 1979). These factors combine to give mixed messages about the overall merit of open admissions, which should be examined carefully.

Collectively, these and other factors have pressured predominantly white institutions to create and/or expand new programs and resources with which to educate and prepare black collegians better than before for careers and leadership roles. Additionally, these programs have resulted in many black students' remaining in college and in some cases have contributed directly to their graduation. Of course, the development of these resources was not without limitations. Never were these programs intended to be a panacea for every problem a black student might face, nor were they designed to let student affairs and academic units abdicate their responsibility to black students. Overall, these factors combined to create black student resources and programs that in many cases remain integral to campuses today. These black student resources vary in focus, size, function, and administration. The various types of black programs and services are listed below.

Types of Black Student Services

Black student services are varied in breadth and depth; they provide support both for graduate and for undergraduate students, and in some cases they extend to precollege students. Several types of black student services may be present on a campus, including special admissions, pre- or postcollege services, orientation, general (academic) studies, financial aid, and black cultural events (Carey, Singh, and Pillinger, 1981). These resources are designed to address black students' academic or intellectual, social, learning, and personal development needs, using learning formats such as peer group instruction, individualized or self-paced learning modules, and direct classroom instruction. In addition, faculty and staff employed in those units frequently are called on to consult with other college staff or faculty regarding black student development needs. Historically, some of these programs were intended to help black students remediate their academic deficiencies so that they could perform competitively with other students. Later black services expanded to include other student affairs functions, such as personal or emotional counseling, career or vocational assessment, advising, and financial aid consultation. Professionals in those units had to be familiar with many campus resources, as often black students came to them for general information regarding available campus resources. Because of their accountability for federal monies, most programs included some evaluation component, which monitored programs and services.

Black student services historically have sought to offer a wide range of services to black students, using a variety of service-delivery formats and techniques. Until recently, there were no professional standards or guidelines for the delivery of such services. In 1986, the Council for the Advancement of Standards for Student Services/Student Development Programs published standards and guidelines for conducting minority student services on campuses (see appendixes 1 and 2, this volume). These standards and guidelines provide directions to administrators as they conduct black and other minority student programs; they offer guidance for services in all areas of operation. Beyond this resource, institutions may consider several suggestions for conducting black student programs and for offering services.

Strategies for Effective Programs

To help black students develop their academic skills fully, institutions must implement services and programs that promote black students' academic, social, and personal development. This goal cannot be accomplished until institutions counteract blacks' alienation through a moral commitment to affirm and practice equal opportunity and human and academic rights in all programs and services (McClain, 1982). The following represent workable suggestions: (1) Programs and services should be well grounded in theory that is culturally appropriate for blacks, (2) programs should be defined by their functional characteristics as well as by status, (3) services and programs should be based on the ethical concept of social justice, which should be reflected in all areas of operation, and (4) programs should emphasize development of students' talent and, as such, should promote independent, critical thinking (Gordon, 1984).

Effective programs for black students begin long before students arrive on campus. University admissions offices must communicate to parents, students, and high schools the institution's interest in the college education of black high school students. To ensure a good match between student and institution, the admissions recruitment process should portray the university's mission, academic curricula, and out-of-classroom opportunities responsibly and honestly. Ensuring this match may involve analyzing students' transcripts and helping students compare the institution's curricular offerings with individual educational goals.

Financial Aid. For students with financial need, providing early information concerning financial aid options and deadlines offers reassurance that recruitment messages are sincere. Parents should receive information at the same time their children do. This suggestion is critical, especially when parents are unfamiliar with the college environment or have low literacy and do not understand application forms.

Developmental Academic Instruction. Academic preassessment and tutorial support are essential to ensure black students' academic success. Among the activities that may support academic development are developmental courses taught by faculty with academic rank; self-paced modules; instructional laboratories; and comprehensive tutorial services. Comprehensive tutoring, small-group and individual, may be considered, especially when it promotes positive peer interactions that enhance academic motivation.

Orientation. One essential program that encourages black student success is a strong orientation program. On-campus orientation activities for parents and students facilitate a positive transition to college life. After students arrive, a primary orientation task is assessment of students' needs through self-report surveys or through other means, to solidify academic, personal, and social goals. Skill-building orientation activities such as time management complement learning and enhance students' confidence in their ability to succeed.

Black Faculty and Staff. Black students need to interact with black staff and faculty members. Black faculty are essential to students as role models, mentors, informal counselors, and advisers. Black faculty provide standards for adult behavior while advising black student organizations, chairing committees to plan activities for special events, presenting workshops on cultural events or black culture, and being responsive to students' academic, social, and developmental needs. The importance of these faculty roles in attracting and retaining black students cannot be overemphasized; institutions must employ blacks at all staffing levels, including in the upper administration.

Of course, not all black faculty are appropriate mentors. Black staff who have assimilated into the majority campus life-style often do not easily or readily interact with black students. Such black staff, like their white counterparts, may benefit from sensitivity training that emphasizes black culture.

The ideal programs provide a mentor for each student participating in a support activity. Faculty and staff members, whether black or white, can become effective with students if they possess good human relations skills and use them to understand students' needs. A role model or mentor cannot always be of the same race as the student but that person must invest personal time in the student's academic and personal growth. If the mentor is white, the mentoring process is a particularly delicate balance between adequate support and scrupulous avoidance of patronizing.

Black Student Resources in Other Student Affairs Programs. Black student services often are found outside traditional black programs. These services, housed among other student affairs units, provide the student with exposure to other campus resources, which may complement their educational objectives. For example, Grinnell College (Iowa) holds fireside lounge lectures for black students. Students are exposed to black community leaders during a series of informal lectures covering black heritage and black peer relationships.

The Dean of Students office at Iowa State University, as a part of its proactive leadership-development programming, asks black students to study black playwrights and their plays. Later, these students produce a play for local residents and students as a way of teaching leadership skills and of enhancing black cultural awareness.

Program Goals. To be successful, a program must have clearly defined goals and objectives and measurable outcomes, regularly evaluated. The program functions must be communicated clearly to the black students it serves and to the entire university community. Whether service are separate or mainstreamed, intrainstructional cooperation is necessary.

Summary

Black students, as a group, are different from their predecessors. They are heterogeneous, and they vary in social class, economic status, values, customs, and family constellations. While on campus, black students receive mixed messages of support. As a result, while they enter with positive aspirations, they too often depart prematurely, without a degree and having felt alone and alienated.

Black students require comprehensive support services, including consultation on admissions, orientation to academic tutoring, and faculty mentoring. These "special services" are intended to help students affirm self-identity. Future programs should direct students toward close involvement with faculty and staff and also should facilitate increased campus interdepartmental cooperation in the development of a campus environment consistent in its support messages to black students.

The ideal program promotes academic excellence in black students through the efforts of highly skilled professionals familiar with students' culture-specific needs, state-of-the-art technology, and high-quality resources. The result of these efforts will be highly skilled black men and women graduates, capable of leading the country into the next century.

References

Astin, A. W. *Achieving Educational Excellence: A Critical Assessment of Priorities and Practices in Higher Education*. San Francisco: Jossey-Bass, 1985.

Carey, P., Singh, B., and Pillinger, B. "Impact: A Summer Enrichment Program for Minority/Disadvantaged Undergraduates at the University of Minnesota." In G. E. Thomas (ed.), *Black Students in Higher Education: Conditions and Experiences in the 1970s*. Westport, Conn.: Greenwood Press, 1981.

Fleming, J. E. "The Opening of White Colleges and Universities to Black Students." In G. E. Thomas (ed.), *Black Students in Higher Education: Conditions and Experiences in the 1970s*. Westport, Conn.: Greenwood Press, 1981.

Fleming, J. *Blacks in College: A Comparative Study of Students' Success in Black and in White Institutions*. San Francisco: Jossey-Bass, 1984.

Gordon, E. W. "The Social and Ethical Context of Special Programs." In S. H. Adolphus (ed.), *Equality Postponed: Continuing Barriers to Higher Education in the 1980s*. New York: College Entrance Examination Board, 1984.

McClain, B. R. "Racism in Higher Education: A Societal Reflection." *The Negro Educational Review*, 1982, *33* (1), 34–45.

Maynard, M. "Can Universities Adapt to Ethnic Minority Students' Needs?" *Journal of College Student Personnel*, 1980, *21* (4), 398–401.

Mingle, J. R. "The Opening of White Colleges and Universities to Black Students." In G. E. Thomas (ed.), *Black Students in Higher Education: Conditions and Experiences in the 1970s*. Westport, Conn.: Greenwood Press, 1981.

Morris, L. *Elusive Equality: The Status of Black Americans in Higher Education*. Washington, D.C.: Howard University Press, 1979.

Scott, W. C. "Critical Factors for the Survival of First Generation College Blacks." In G. E. Thomas (ed.), *Black Students in Higher Education: Conditions and Experiences in the 1970s*. Westport, Conn.: Greenwood Press, 1981.

Stikes, C. S. *Black Students in Higher Education*. Carbondale: Southern Illinois University Press, 1984.

Thomas, G. E. (ed.) *Black Students in Higher Education: Conditions and Experiences in the 1970s*. Westport, Conn.: Greenwood Press, 1981.

Tinto, V. "Dropout from Higher Education: A Theoretical Synthesis of Recent Research." *Review of Educational Research*, 1975, *45* (1), 89–125.

Willie, C. V., and McCord, A. S. *Black Students at White Colleges*. New York: Praeger, 1972.

Wright, D. J. "Orienting Minority Students." In M. L. Upcraft (ed.), *Orienting Students to College*. New Directions for Student Services, no. 25. San Francisco: Jossey-Bass, 1984.

Augustine W. Pounds is dean of students at Iowa State University. She has been active in minority student services for several years.

To reach full potential, practitioners must challenge themselves
to outreach to Asian American students and reflect their
cultures' rich diversity in high-quality programs and services.

Asian American College Student Perspectives

Charlene A. Chew, Alan Yoshiharu Ogi

Asian American students experience unique struggles, living a multicultural existence. Having one foot embedded in American values and the other foot in Asian values provides a richness and depth that a monocultural experience lacks. This chapter discusses the learning, social, and emotional needs of Asian American college students and portrays that multicultural existence as a challenge for student affairs practitioners. Several strategies for developing programs and services are recommended.

Asian American students are identified by different terms or phrases: *Asian–Pacific Islander, Asian American*. A few insensitive people will use the term *Oriental*, which is believed to be covertly racist and is not acceptable to many Asian students. Asian American students are from such countries of origin as China, India, Japan, Korea, the Pacific Islands, the Philippines, and Southeast Asia. Each ethnic group has distinct subcultures, involving unique values and customs.

On college campuses, one finds Asian students who are foreign-born and those who are American-born. Except for indigenous Hawaiians, all Asian American groups immigrated to the United States (Suzuki, 1983). Those ethnic groups that immigrated include Asian Indians, Chinese, Filipinos, Guamanians, Japanese, Koreans, Samoans, and Vietnamese (Suzuki, 1983).

D. J. Wright (ed.). *Responding to the Needs of Today's Minority Students.*
New Directions for Student Services, no. 38. San Francisco: Jossey-Bass, Summer 1987.

In the 1840s, the Chinese were the first Asians to arrive in the United States. The Japanese followed, arriving between 1890 and 1924. In smaller numbers, Korean immigrants first appeared in the United States around 1903. Koreans were not to immigrate again until after World War II and the Korean Conflict. Filipinos, in 1934, were among the last Asians to come to the United States during this first immigration phase (Suzuki, 1983). Most early immigrants were poor farmers, laborers, and peasants. Between 1934 and 1965, the United States permitted no immigration from Asia (Suzuki, 1983). Since 1965, Asian immigrants have arrived from Vietnam, Kampuchea (Cambodia), and other Southeast Asian countries. The most recent Southeast Asian immigrants have been refugees of varying economic classes and backgrounds. At universities, especially those on the West Coast, it is not uncommon to find Asian American students from several of these ethnic groups in the student population.

As reported by Suzuki (1983), the 1980 census showed persons of Asian and Pacific Island background increased from 1 million in 1970 to over 3.5 million in 1980—an increase of 128 percent. During this same time, black populations increased by 17 percent, Hispanic by 61 percent, and American Indian by 71 percent. Suzuki concludes that Asian American population growth was almost double that of the next fastest-growing minority and more than ten times that of the U.S. population as a whole.

Prejudice and Discrimination

Asian Americans have a long history as victims of racism and discrimination. It began with the arrival of the first Chinese in the 1840s; it continues with the present immigration of Southeast Asian refugees. Today racism and discrimination appear to stem from naive and misinformed attitudes reinforced by insensitive educators; increased public attention to the impact of Asian industries on the U.S. economy, and media exploitation. These beliefs and practices have contributed to renewed prejudice and violence against Asian Americans.

Misconceptions about Asian Americans have been perpetuated by the ever-popular Kung Fu movie craze. Movies such as *Year of the Dragon*, highlighting violent Chinatown gangs, *Karate Kid*, depicting an elderly Japanese man pruning his bonsai tree while imparting ultimate wisdom, and *Gung Ho*, portraying an overly disciplined Asian American being "saved" by a "mellow American," exhibit stereotypes and perpetuate prejudices toward Asians and Asian Americans. In extreme contrast, films such as *The Gold Watch*, portraying the hardship of a first generation of (*Issei*) Japanese farmer struggling during the evacuation to an American concentration camp, *Dim Sum*, focusing on a modern-day Chinese American woman and the value differences she confronts, and *Hata Hito, Raise the Banner*, highlighting the life of Japanese immigrants, communicate the richness and struggles of the Asian American experience.

What remain untold are accounts of the recent, real-life assaults on Asian American men, women, and children by frightened, angry, and mis-educated non-Asians. The media fail to report the real and traumatic incidents with the same vigor expended on promotion of the aforementioned movies; consequently, Asian Americans' cultural values and traditions are distorted, and their persecution by racists goes unrecognized.

Student affairs professionals working with Asian and Asian American students must avoid perpetuating misconceptions and should guard against viewing Asian Americans as a homogeneous group. If such distortions infiltrate services and activities, a campus climate may develop in which Asian American students and their accomplishments are ignored, denigrated, or devalued. Such a climate undermines students' development and academic progress. Practitioners should review all written and audio and visual resources carefully for stated or implied biases. Staff training may be necessary for professionals to recognize and alter such biases.

Values of Asian Americans

Asian American students often are confused by the conflict between their cultural values and U.S. ideals. American ideals and values, especially those found in institutions of higher education, are quite different from those found in Asian cultures. Asian value systems derive from the feudal teachings of Confucianism and Taoism, and include a secondary role for women and an emphasis on the group through filial piety, humility, restraint of emotional expression, and sense of obligation. These teachings in turn support the idea that women play a secondary role in society (Homma-True, 1980). In many Asian cultures, the family name is engendered by the male, and the female is considered less important. This practice is derived from the earlier belief that women were commodities, rather than independent, rational thinkers. In contrast to Western philosophy, which holds to the development and survival of the individual, these feudal teachings prescribe a structure for family order and encourage hierarchical thinking, which centers on the group. The family is most valued, and individual worth is based on interdependence and collective (group) worth.

Filial Piety. This concept refers to the total devotion of children to the family, and it is highly prized in Asian American culture. Conformity to this obligation is encouraged by the manipulation of guilt and shame in lieu of direct punitive action. This concept can easily be perceived as incongruent with a university's goal of promoting critical thinking or team building.

Humility. This quality is valued above the boisterous, assertive behaviors one might expect from energetic college students on U.S. campuses. From this societal value comes the image of the quiet, shy, and introverted Asian American student, who may have little to add to the fast-paced, action-oriented dynamics of many campus activities.

Restraint of Emotional Expression. Refraining from expression of strong feelings and controlling one's will are important values for many Asian Americans. Free expression of feelings in conflict situations is not encouraged; restraint, it is believed, allows the individual to resolve the conflict inwardly and avoids immediate outbursts, which are seen as detrimental and embarassing to the family.

Sense of Obligation. Interpersonal relationships may be seen as obligations. Asian American students, exposed to U.S. dating customs, may believe it is all right to search for a suitable partner without input from parents, but traditional Asian American parents or grandparents may still expect to select friends and spouses for their sons or daughters according to standards of ethnicity, background, and family.

Asian American Diversity

Asian American diversity results not only from different national and cultural backgrounds but also from intergenerational barriers, whether the student is American-born or foreign-born.

First, with each generation there are changes in traditional values, but this does not remove intergenerational conflicts. The first-generation Asian American emigrated for socioeconomic or political opportunities, seeking in the United States prosperity, employment, and security, but traditional cultural values often remained intact. The second-generation Asian American is usually the first naturalized United States citizen. Often persons of the second generation experience conflicting devotion to two value systems. Assimilation and acculturation as means of social acceptance are suspect to this generation. Cultural diversity may be first encountered, in terms of social development and skills in communication and group interactions, only when the second-generation Asian American enters college. The third-generation Asian American adopts more American values than the previous generations; however, he or she retains some traditional values, such as a tendency toward introspection, respect for cultural heritage, and reverence for elders. Successive generations continue to be more acculturated into the American mainstream, but traditional Asian values remain.

Second, American-born and foreign-born Asians often have little in common. Moreover, American-born Asians may shun the foreign-born because the former are reminded that they should have greater interest in their Asian countries of origin. The politics of some Asian countries may cause first-generation Asian Americans to fear that family members who have not emigrated are in danger in their homeland. Often, these fears are realistic.

On some campuses, these issues promote interactions between foreign-born and American-born Asians, while on other campuses they generate friction and disagreement. New issues develop with each wave of Asian immigration to the United States. Student affairs professionals, if they are to work effectively, need to recognize the roles of history and values for Asian American students.

Interventions to Facilitate Academic and Personal Development

Institutions should develop services and programs that enhance Asian American students' success. Assessment is an important first step. Student affairs professionals should consider the following variables when planning programs and services for Asian American students.

- Asian American student population size
- Identities of specific Asian American student groups, clubs, or organizations
- Descriptions of interaction patterns among Asian American student groups
- Identification of areas where Asian American groups congregate
- Common points of Asian American student groups
- Identities of cultural heritage, and generational groups' activities
- Study of student services' communication with minority groups
- Review of previous Asian American student services
- Active involvement of Asian American parents
- Understanding of past and present Asian American involvement with university administration.

From the information acquired from the assessment of these variables, practitioners can develop high-quality programs and services, such as the following, for Asian American students.

Participation in College and Community Organizations. Asian American students participate in many college and community organizations. Ideally, such contacts provide an opportunity to interact with individuals who share similar values, a sense of validation in the personal struggle for college achievement, and models for success in the campus setting. Practitioners working with Asian American students should know about such student resources and how they are utilized as social support systems.

In addition, one should be aware of where student groups typically meet. One group may meet in the library, another in a particular food-service area, while yet a third may select a room in the student union. Such information tells practitioners how to reach and communicate with particular groups.

A general type of social club is the Asian American student union. Within such a club, individuals attain a sense of belonging and develop leadership skills. Socially, unions use banquets and activities such as dances and athletic tournaments to create togetherness. Other extended ventures of student unions may include offering discounted vacation trips, doing educational programming, and providing job placement and assistance.

One special type of social club has religious affiliations. Christian groups seem to be the major religious clubs formed on campuses. Many Asian countries were influenced greatly by Christian missionaries. Each Asian American ethnic group may form its own religious organization, but it is not uncommon for other Asian American students to be included. Church or community groups may form away from campus and be used to promote social interaction and relationships among students.

While an ethnic mix in social clubs has its advantages, it can cause splinter factions, which sap the organization's effectiveness. Splintering is not uncommon in groups attracting both American-born and foreign-born Asians. Background and language differences contribute to these intragroup conflicts, which may require the intervention of student affairs professionals for successful resolution.

Participation in Social Activities. Among other social activities that appeal to Asian American students, especially those on the West Coast, are skiing, dances, casino nights, cultural food events, Asian American film and media festivals, and celebrations such as Chinese New Year and the Cherry Blossom Festival. Asian American art exhibits and remembrances of historical events (Japanese American concentration camps, the dropping of the A-bomb on Hiroshima and Nagasaki) are also examples of student programming. Large-scale Asian American student events on campus may be offered in conjunction with other campus-sponsored events, depending on the size and depth of the university's population. Although these programs are like those already found on campuses, their focus on the culture and heritage of Asian Americans further validates an Asian American student's view of the world.

Development of Student Leadership. Professionals should understand the leadership within student organizations, for it reveals much regarding group dynamics and social or political orientation. There may be groups that select isolation from other Asian American groups because of long-standing antagonism. Other groups have leaders whose main interest is social interaction with other Asian Americans. These groups must address the question of acceptance or rejection by those outside their own Asian American ethnic group and by the non-Asian population.

As with other groups, an Asian American group needs to have an overriding theme so that a sense of purpose can emerge. Student affairs professionals may play a useful role by helping Asian American student organizations ascertain their needs, establish order, identify purposes, and set goals. In the process, student affairs professionals acquire valuable information regarding programs for Asian American students.

Professionals should begin working with Asian American groups by communicating with the leaders first, because recognition within Asian American groups is measured by one's acceptance by an established group member. Professionals can inform leaders of their services and solicit their input into the development of future services. If possible, this initial contact should be made by an Asian American staff member who is sensitive to the pulse of the Asian American student community. If no Asian American professional staff person is available, one might seek an Asian American paraprofessional or student to act as liaison. Under no circumstances should student affairs professionals abdicate work with Asian American students. The reality is that white professionals will have to learn to work with Asian American students because it is an essential part of their responsibility. Student affairs professionals must establish credibility with and demonstrate sensitivity to Asian American students. Many times an Asian American paraprofessional may help to bridge the differences, especially if the student affairs office has a history of little involvement with Asian Americans.

A primary requirement for the liaison is the ability to evoke and maintain student trust. Employing an Asian American staff person may not be enough to demonstrate trust. If that person is not accepted by students or is unwilling or unable to interact with them effectively, then the entire program suffers. To assume that Asian American ancestry in and of itself qualifies an otherwise unqualified person is just as prejudicial as the converse assumption. Ideally, liaisons and advisers to Asian American student groups will be sensitive, knowledgeable people who have excellent public speaking and organizational planning skills and who come from varying Asian American cultural backgrounds and value orientations. They will elicit trust and respect while allowing students some choice of perspective and experience.

Participation of Family. The family is an important part of Asian American culture. Student affairs professionals need to recognize, explore, and create methods for Asian American parents to assist and support their children on campus. Some families are newly immigrated. To them, college programs are unfamiliar and often intimidating. A family adjusting to changing roles, different work-styles, long work hours, language barriers, fear of an unknown (campus) environment, and possibly unemployment may not respond readily to students' college needs. Under better circumstances, or with sufficient support and understanding from the student affairs professional, Asian American families can take great pride and interest in their children's achievement, although the language barrier may pose problems to their active participation in some programs. In developing support activities that involve parents, it is important to assess the range of family circumstances and needs and then to design programs responsive to the parental need continuum presented by the student population.

Participation in Leadership Development Seminars. Leadership seminars are an excellent way to teach leadership skills to Asian American students while providing opportunities for group interaction. Students first learn to engage in small talk and then progress from disclosing personal information to informative talk, finally mastering persuasive talk. Additionally, leadership seminars help student groups acquire solid organizational and communication skills, which enable organizations to coexist in a supportive campus community.

In developing leaders, student affairs professionals should attend to personal development skills while helping students recognize political and social realities. Important factors to address are the following personal and social issues: managing cultural and family intragroup conflict, cultural pride, cultural knowledge, real and perceived racial oppression, student government funding, political unrest (in an Asian country), academic acceptance, and self-awareness.

Student affairs professionals should involve community leaders and other community resources in the leadership training sessions. Asian American writers, filmmakers, and educators might be included, as well as other professionals whose leadership skills can enhance self- and group awareness among Asian American students. Nurturing these students' cultural curiosity can make the university's student affairs programs highly effective.

Collaboration with Asian American Studies Departments. An Asian American studies department provides an important campus network for student affairs professionals. Asian American students may enroll in Asian American studies to advance their understanding of their own cultural backgrounds. Student affairs professionals involved with these academic units can reach many Asian American students by sponsoring programs on Asian American issues, such as redress and reparation for Japanese Americans, the political turmoil of the Philippines, and the expanding commercial enterprises of the People's Republic of China.

Asian American studies programs have enormous potential for fostering self-esteem and self-validation among Asian American students. Such programs legitimize students' campus and community roles. They also provide student affairs professionals with the knowledge and skills necessary to interact more successfully with Asian American students. Outreach presentations in academic classes improve this linkage and inform students and faculty of available services.

Publication of Newsletters. An excellent communications link among Asian American students is a campus newsletter. Newsletters or weekly bulletins provide vital information and give students a forum in which to express their opinions. Newsletters should use commonly recognized Asian American words or phrases that have special meanings for students. Involvement of Asian American students in the publication process keeps the link meaningful and genuine for the readers. Distribution should be focused on the observed gathering areas of Asian American students.

Asian American students are frequently concerned about identity and the Asian American experience. The student affairs staff can help only if they are well informed about current resources and teaching methods. Asian American resources centers, bookstores, and libraries are good places to start learning. There is an Asian American film company, based in Los Angeles, that has films and videos that speak to the Asian American experience, and there are some television programs, theatrical groups, and community programs that focus specifically on Asian American issues.

A university needs to conduct an inventory of the Asian American resources available and, if necessary, bring in more sources from outside. If there are Asian or Asian American students on campus, the student affairs staff must provide the support and services necessary for them to succeed in college.

Development of Role Models. Asian American students, like all students, benefit from appropriate role models. Students from the "Sixties Generation" are now adults who have moved into the mainstream and can serve as role models for today's Asian American students. Examples of such models are the young Asian American attorneys for Japanese-American Redress and Reparations Litigation. While second-, third-, or fourth-generation Chinese, Japanese, or Korean Americans generally are not involved in protest marches, they often do participate in remembrances and cultural parades, thus promoting political change "within the system." This method of promoting change seems to affirm the acculturation of the Asian American population today. If and how one decides to acculturate appears to be a developmental issues of prime importance to today's young Asian American students; role models facilitate resolution of that issue.

Intergroup Acceptance

Perceived differences and divisions exist between Asian American groups and assessment of their needs and the best methods for meeting those needs on campus. Too many professionals still assume—wrongly—that a person who is "Asian" will get along with all other Asian Americans. To correct this erroneous attitude, the student affairs professional needs a more informed understanding of the historical relationships between and among various Asian American cultural groups.

The most significant historical event influencing Asian American groups occurred during World War II, when the former Empire of Japan ravaged Asian and South Pacific areas. War atrocities endured by nations opposing Japan are the source of many prejudices and well-concealed hatreds. These perceptions, beliefs, and experiences continue to affect intergroup relations today as they are passed on to children and grandchildren.

In the planning of group activities, historical data are useful guides. Most Asian American second-, third-, or fourth-generation citizens realize that Japanese Americans were not involved in the Japanese atrocities during the Second World War; nevertheless, this single issue illustrates how important it is that practitioners know and understand historical perspectives and avoid erroneous and counterproductive generalizations.

Conclusion

This chapter has provided an informed description of Asian Americans, with the purpose of eradicating the myth that they are a successful or "model" minority group. Clearly, Asian Americans desire to reach their full potential in college, independent of campus constraints and cultural biases. Institutions that have the greatest success in educating Asian Americans have recognized specific cultural group needs by developing relevant programs and services. Continued success among all institutions in responding to Asian Americans' academic and social needs can be achieved by involving skilled professionals in high-quality, sensitive programs for Asian American students. The completion of such goals will result in the expansion of Asian Americans into all areas of campus life, which benefits the student, the family, the institution, faculty, and staff.

References

Homma-True, R. "Mental Health Issues Among Asian American Women." In National Institute of Education (ed.), *Conference on the Educational and Occupational Needs of Asian/Pacific American Women.* Washington, D.C.: U.S. Government Printing Office, 1980.

Suzuki, B. H. "The Education of Asian and Pacific Americans: An Introductory Overview." In D. T. Nakanishi and M. Hirano-Nakanishi (eds.), *The Education of Asian and Pacific Americans: Historical Perspectives and Prescriptions for the Future.* Phoenix, Ariz.: Oryx Press, 1983.

Charlene A. Chew is associate director of residential life at San Jose University.

Alan Yoshiharu Ogi is residence hall director and lecturer at San Jose University.

While U.S. Hispanics are purported to be among the fastest-growing population groups in the nation, their growth will be realized when colleges devise innovative approaches to Hispanic student programs and services.

Facilitating the Development of Hispanic College Students

Ennio L. Quevedo-García

The Challenge of the Future

The decade of the nineties will be one of challenge for administrators, counselors, and teachers charged with facilitating the educational development of the nation's fastest-growing population—Hispanics. According to the 1980 U.S. census, the estimated Hispanic population of 14.6 million represents a ten-year increase of slightly over 60 percent, compared to a total population increase of only 11 percent. U.S. Hispanics tend to be younger than the general population. In 1982 the median age of Hispanics was 23.7 years, while that of the non-Hispanic population was 31.0 years. About 11 percent of all Hispanics are under 5 years of age, as compared to 7 percent of the non-Hispanic population (U.S. Department of Commerce, 1985).

The Term **Hispanic.** *Hispanic* is the current collective label used by the U.S. government to refer to the individuals of a group that includes Mexican/Chicano (60 percent), Puerto Ricans (14 percent), Cuban Americans (6 percent), and other Hispanics (20 percent). While there has been much debate about the appropriateness of this designation, for the purposes of this chapter *Hispanic* will be used to refer to U.S. citizens whose countries of ethnic origin were colonized by Spain and are now Spanish-

D. J. Wright (ed.). *Responding to the Needs of Today's Minority Students.*
New Directions for Student Services, no. 38. San Francisco: Jossey-Bass, Summer 1987.

speaking. It will not be used to refer to international students from Spanish-speaking countries. Although I recognize the artificiality of the term *Hispanic,* I shall use it here when referring to this population in general; comments related to specific Hispanic subgroups will be so noted.

Hispanic Diversity. In the 1960s and the 1970s, when Hispanic students were making a substantial debut on our college campuses, well-meaning college practitioners tended to relate to them as one homogeneous group. It is not surprising that this approach proved inadequate. The Hispanic population is made up of citizens whose origins can be traced to over twenty-five separate Spanish-speaking nations. Hispanics are black, white, Asian American, American Indian, or a mixture of any of the four; thus, there is no validity to any racial tag that might be applied to the population. Also, there is no single political or religious philosophy that can be pointed to as being common to U.S. Hispanics, nor is there any one economic class in which they are not represented. Each of the populations has its own history, demographic patterns, language variations, and perception of its niche in the U.S. sociological structure (Ford Foundation, 1984). Except for politicized individuals, most Hispanics use their specific nationalities (that is, Mexican American, Chicano, Puerto Rican, Cuban American, and so forth) when identifying themselves.

However, in spite of this variety, U.S. Hispanics themselves recognize a common definable Hispanic culture that exists in the United States. In a recent study, 78 percent of the Hispanics surveyed agreed with the following statement: "Although Hispanics living in the United States trace their roots back to many Latin American countries, there is still a common denominator of Hispanic culture in the United States, especially for Hispanics in the same socioeconomic class" (Grossman, 1984).

The Challenge. Currently, only 8 percent of the total U.S. Hispanic population has completed four years or more of college, compared to 18 percent of the non-Hispanic population (U.S. Department of Commerce, 1985). Certainly, numerous factors contribute to this discrepancy, but student affairs practitioners cannot cite the multiplicity of sources as an excuse for their programs' shortcomings. If practitioners are to be successful in structuring environments that will help Hispanic college students develop to their full potential as individuals, they must more fully understand and appreciate the various cultural, economic, social, and political backgrounds that these students bring with them to our campuses. Without that understanding and appreciation, practitioners will remain naive and will fail to retain Hispanics on their campuses.

A Historical Perspective

Diversity has been a common theme in the historical development of the Hispanic cultural groups that trace their precursors to the continents of Europe, Africa, and Asia. For eight hundred years, from 711 to 1492, Spain was both ruled and culturally influenced by Moorish Northern Africa, which contributed greatly to the development of the Spanish culture in science, language, architecture, mathematics, and law. In fact, much of what is considered typically Hispanic actually is directly transplanted from Africa. It was during these eight hundred years, while Christian Spain struggled to "reconquer" the Iberian Peninsula, that Spain became a unified political entity. During this time the regional language of the Castile province became the dominant language of the country, and in 1492, Elio Antonio de Nebrija wrote a Castilian grammar, the first formal grammar ever written for any European language. Today, Castilian, which is more commonly known as Spanish, is the language spoken in over twenty-five countries, with the United States being the fourth-largest Spanish-speaking country in the world (Naisbitt, 1984).

When Cristóbal Colón (Christopher Columbus) successfully crossed the Atlantic Ocean in 1492, he brought the cultural "menus" of Europe and Africa into contact with Asia. According to current anthropological evidence, Asia is the continent of origin of the American Indian peoples, who crossed from Siberia to Alaska around 25,000 B.C. (Wolf, 1972). These highly developed American indigenous societies contributed greatly to the modern cultures of Hispanic America. Like all the other Hispanic cultural contributors, American Indians influenced Hispanic language variations, food, art, and social structures.

During the Spanish colonial period, before slavery was abolished, Africans from many tribes were sent forcibly to the Caribbean regions of the Spanish American Empire. Their influence is alive today, both in the physical appearance and in the cultural expressions of contemporary Latin American cultures.

As the various Latin American nations achieved their independence, immigration was encouraged in order to facilitate settlement of rural areas. As a result, today in Latin America one will find descendants of immigrants from every world nation, and, as in the United States, many of these Hispanic individuals function in the mainstream of their adopted nations yet maintain the cultural practices of their original nationalities.

Although many Hispanics either immigrated or were descendants of U.S. immigrants from Latin American nations, it would be incorrect to assume that all U.S. Hispanics are of immigrant stock. For many Hispanics, U.S. citizenship was the result of U.S. expansionist activities, such as the Mexican War, which resulted in the transfer of the modern-day states of Texas, Colorado, New Mexico, Arizona, Nevada, and California from Mexico to the United States with the signing of the Treaty of Guadalupe Hidalgo in 1848. This is also true for Puerto Rican Hispanics, who found their homeland ceded to the United States after the Spanish American War (Herring, 1967). U.S. citizenship was granted to the inhabitants of Puerto

Rico in 1917. It is important to note that as a result of the unique histories of Mexican and Puerto Rican Hispanics, their political perspectives regarding their relationship to the United States may differ greatly from those of other Hispanic students.

Issues in Working with Hispanic Students

Because of this multiplicity of social, cultural, and economic backgrounds, practitioners working with Hispanic students face a number of complicated issues, the resolution of which requires research-based program designs that consider the heterogeneity of this student population.

Assimilation Versus Integration. A concrete decision regarding adaptive responses to increased interaction with the dominant U.S. culture is a challenge faced by every Hispanic college student, regardless of cultural or socioeconomic background. According to Berry (1980), individuals can opt for one of four strategies to reduce acculturative conflict: rejection, deculturation, assimilation, or integration. The first two, rejection and deculturation, are adaptive responses utilized by individuals who view interaction between the dominant society and members of their own culture as something negative, something to be avoided. By seeking admission into college, Hispanic students logically eliminate their opportunity for utilizing these first two options. Assimilation, or relinquishing one's cultural identity and moving into the larger society, is the option taken by students who view relations with the dominant culture as positive and the maintenance of their cultural identity as being of no value. Integration, in contrast, implies that an individual values both movement toward becoming an integral part of the larger societal framework and maintenance of cultural identity.

It would be unethical for a practitioner to influence a Hispanic student's choice between integration or assimilation as an acculturative response. The right to decide on one's own identity must lie with the individual. It is important, however, that professionals recognize this decision-making process as a valid step in the student's total development and that they provide the information and environment necessary for such a decision. In order to decide on the value of either one's own or the dominant culture, the Hispanic student needs to be exposed to as many aspects of each as possible. For Hispanic students with little or no experience of Anglo culture, opportunities for exposure need to be provided. Perhaps the best way to facilitate this exposure is to structure informal interactions between Anglo and Hispanic students on college campuses.

The more acute need in this area, however, seems to be that of providing Hispanic students with information about their own culture. Academic courses in Hispanic language, literature, history, art, and sociopolitical issues should be available to students. Opportunities for students should be provided to organize and produce, for the entire college community, cultural events such as art shows, dances, film festivals, or lectures. In his general recommendations regarding minorities in the higher-education setting, Astin (1982) wrote that colleges and universities should provide resources to establish centers where minority students can meet for social and educational exchanges. Such centers, he argued, could promote a system to foster cultural identity, pride, and strength in such a way that minority students would be able to challenge as well as enrich and broaden the traditional values of the institution.

Whatever the acculturative responses chosen by Hispanic students, these students are likely to encounter individuals at home and in the college environment who will challenge their choices. The dissonance produced by these challenges, although emotionally painful, is an important step in students' identity development. Professionals who work with Hispanics should be able to recognize this process and be prepared to provide the counseling and support necessary to facilitate students' progress through this stage.

Ties to Family and Community. Traditional Hispanic culture is family- and community-oriented. Students who come from this type of environment may view themselves as representatives of their communities and family units first and as individuals second. Individualism in traditional Hispanic familial units is not stressed to the degree that it is in Anglo cultures. In Grossman's (1984) study, 90 percent of Hispanics surveyed agreed with the statement that "Hispanics have a strong identification with and loyalty to their family and community. They are brought up to believe that contributing to and sacrificing for the benefit of the group is more important than personal aggrandizement. As a result, Hispanic students may feel highly motivated to do things that have significance for their families, friends, and community."

Major life decisions, such as college attendance, are usually made with the consultation and blessing of other family members. This process has implications for the success of the Hispanic college student. Regardless of socioeconomic background, if the student is the product of a home environment that places a positive value on formal education, that student is likely to experience less stress throughout the transition into college life because of familial suppport and positive reinforcement.

For the practitioner, a knowledge of the individual Hispanic student's home environment is an important tool that can be utilized in deciding on individual counseling strategies. Families of students who are products of educationally supportive environments take ownership in the student's success and should be involved in the counseling process as much as possible. In order to do this, institutions must develop significant programs that familiarize Hispanic parents and siblings with the college setting and provide them with the opportunity to meet and develop a rapport with college educators and staff members.

When the Hispanic student's home environment does not provide positive reinforcement for educational pursuits, the student must learn to cope with the stress involved in forsaking the wishes of family in order to attain personal educational goals. In this case, it may be helpful to identify campus resources that can provide the needed support. Interested Hispanic faculty or staff members, Hispanic student organizations, or campus clergy might be utilized. In either case, lack of knowledge of the individual student's home environment can become a major handicap to facilitating success in college.

College Choice. As with all college students, factors such as cost, availability of desired programs, geographical location, mission of the institution, available facilities, student body, curriculum offerings, curriculum requirements, image, reputation, and administrative procedures influence the student's propensity to enroll in and successfully graduate from a given institution (Beal and Noel, 1984). According to Durán (1983), factors such as the economic needs of students' families, the expectation of parents about their children's education, and the sociocultural influence of students' communities and peer networks affect Hispanics' decisions and choices for college candidacy. For many Hispanic students, cost and geographical location have special significance for deciding on enrollment in a given institution.

Cost and Location. High cost and low availability of funds continue to present barriers to Hispanics who desire college educations. According to recent U.S. Census Bureau publications, Hispanic average income on the West Coast, where 7.9 million of the nation's Hispanics reside, fell by 5 percent last year, while the poverty rate rose to 26 percent, six percentage points higher than the poverty rate for Western blacks (Schreiner, 1986). As government financial aid programs disappear and alternative sources of funding (such as scholarships, private loans, and student work opportunities) become more scarce, the outlook for substantial increases in Hispanic college enrollments is bleak. Given larger families and smaller median incomes (U.S. Department of Commerce, 1985), disproportionately higher numbers of Hispanics than whites will be denied access to college education in the 1990s, simply because it is unaffordable. Perhaps the most significant test of an institution's receptivity to the presence of Hispanic and other minority students is the quality and quantity of financial assistance that an institution makes available to them.

When cost becomes the overriding factor in the choice of a college, other important elements, such as availability of desired curriculum and institutional reputation, become secondary. Inadequate funding may explain the comparatively higher percentage of Hispanic students enrolled in two-year institutions. In the fall of 1978, 42 percent of Hispanic college students were enrolled in two-year colleges, as compared to 23 percent of white non-Hispanic students (Durán, 1983).

Because of the traditional Hispanic's strong identification with and loyalty to the family, geographical location tends to be an important factor in deciding on a college or a university. To many Hispanic parents, giving their blessing to their offspring's desire to attend college in a remote location may seem like shirking parental responsibility. Likewise, a student who decides to attend school elsewhere than in the local community may suffer feelings of guilt at having "abandoned" the family. Significant numbers of Hispanic parents have little concrete knowledge of higher education; their fear of the unknown and their strong cultural impetus to protect their children from negative experiences can lead them to discourage their children from seeking admission to schools offering high-quality programs, simply because they are too far away.

The Entire Family. The key strategy in dealing with the factor of physical and psychological distance as a barrier to Hispanic enrollment is the development of a more personalized recruitment process, which can take into account the information needs of the entire family, not just those of the student. Along with identifying, recruiting, and matriculating Hispanic students, admissions and orientation staff persons must devise processes through which they can educate parents and siblings to the experiences that their loved ones will undergo. The family needs to become comfortable with and trusting of higher education. This change will take time and astute strategic planning. The one-day visit to campus may not suffice for Hispanic families. The familial education process must begin early, perhaps as early as junior high school.

For this process to be successful, managers of orientation and admissions officers first must hire staff members who can relate to Hispanic families. Spanish-speaking staff will be necessary to the success of such programs, since many Hispanic parents, although conversant in English, express themselves more comfortably in Spanish. Also, there are many parents who speak only Spanish. Spanish-speaking student affairs professionals should view their bilingualism as a marketable skill and insist on compensation for their ability to function in more than one cultural arena.

The Precollege Experience. The quality of the Hispanic student's home, school, and community experiences will influence chances for successful matriculation into college (Durán, 1983). The basic ingredient of a healthy precollege experience is sound academic preparation in language, science, and math skills. If students are to develop intellectual competency, they need to enter college settings with the confidence necessary to compete on an equal basis with non-Hispanic peers (Chickering, 1969). Fortunately, the current trend among elementary educators seems to be toward renewed emphasis on the "basics." Early and continuous assessment of student's mastery of these skills, through the use of bias-free instruments, helps guarantee that Hispanic students will not enter college lacking the academic preparation needed to excel.

Aside from adequate academic preparation, substantial information regarding career options should become part of the Hispanic student's elementary, middle, and high school experience. For students to be able to make sound choices regarding educational preparation and career paths, they must become aware of trends in the service and technological industries that affect their potential for future success.

This responsibility should lie not only with the schools but also the communities. Representatives from various professions should be solicited to visit young Hispanics and inform them about their particular disciplines. Whenever possible, mentoring programs between Hispanic high school students and members of the professional community should be established. Youth-oriented civic organizations can serve as a valuable resource in structuring these programs. As early as possible, Hispanic young people need to be taught to plan their futures. They need to be challenged to decide about where they want to see themselves five or ten years after college graduation, and they need to be given the information and planning skills to reach their goals. An early start toward clarifying one's purpose will most certainly facilitate the total developmental process (Chickering, 1969).

If Hispanic students are to function in competitive Anglo-dominated college environments, they must arrive on campus with highly developed assertiveness skills. Traditional Hispanic culture regards assertive behaviors as rude and dishonorable, especially when directed toward elders. In Grossman's (1984) study, 82 percent of Hispanics surveyed agreed with the statement that "Hispanics were less likely to state their disagreement with others or their unwillingness to do what others ask or expect from them." This belief was especially true for children and adolescents who were taught to respect their elders (p. 91). Success in college requires that students feel comfortable with their ability to participate in intellectual debate and discourse, both with other students and with professors. Precollege training in the arts of assertiveness and debate can be most helpful in developing self-esteem and integrity (Chickering, 1969).

Inroads Incorporated: A Model Program

A model program that provides precollege experiences in supplemental academics, skill training, career exposure, and academic counseling is Inroads Incorporated, a nonprofit corporation headquartered in St. Louis, Missouri, with twenty-six affiliates in cities across the country. It exists for the purpose of identifying potentially successful black, Hispanic, and American Indian students and preparing them for eventual positions of leadership in corporate America and in communities.

Since its inception in 1970, Inroads, in partnership with major U.S. corporations, has been successful in placing over seven hundred graduates in management positions in 731 major U.S. corporations. These results were achieved through a very sophisticated process of identifying students with potential through the use of a targeted selection-recruitment process; providing them with ongoing career, personal, and academic counseling during their years in college; working closely with liaisons in sponsoring corporations to structure meaningful, goal-oriented summer work experiences; and providing competency-based training in personal development, career planning, college skills, and corporate survival. The philosophical foundation of Inroads is centered on the belief that the U.S. minority-student community contains as much talent and potential for success as the majority (white) student community. The major goal of Inroads is to facilitate development of that potential.

Inroads looks at many factors when selecting students for its pre-college program: academic record, participation in student organizations, leadership experience, commitment to personal development, support in the home environment, community commitment, and soundness of ethnic identity. Since the goal of the program is to facilitate the personal and academic development of its students, the focus during the selection process is on the search for potential and not on a finished product.

On Saturdays during the academic year and on weekdays during the summer, precollege participants are given supplemental academic instruction in math, science, and language. The curriculum is designed to supplement and enhance the instruction that students receive in class. Specific class content is upwardly graduated so that precollege seniors are exposed to college entry–level content in order to reduce their initial shock of adjustment to college work.

In addition to the academic enhancement experiences, program participants are required to attend monthly counseling sessions with counseling staff. During these sessions, academic progress is reviewed and action plans for improvement are designed, as needed. Individual tutors are provided for students who are not performing well in class.

As part of the precollege experience, students are provided with career-exploration activities designed to give them information regarding career options. These career activities include field trips to local corporate physical plants, visits by local employers, and structured workshops. Students are also provided with technical assistance in choosing and gaining admission to colleges and universities.

The Inroads precollege and college programs owe their success to their focus on the three critical developmental areas: competence, purpose, and identity (Chickering, 1969). In 1985, 61 percent of Inroads precollege participants graduated from high school, were accepted into college, and won four-year internships with major corporations. In that same year, 67 percent of Inroads college participants graduated from college and accepted management positions with their sponsoring companies. Longitudinal studies of the retention of Inroads graduates in their corporations are in progress.

Factors Influencing College Success

It is difficult to identify positive correlations between specific socio-economic characteristics of the general Hispanic population and their negative or positive relationship to chances for educational attainment. This difficulty is due to the differences one finds among these characteristics when examining the various Hispanic subpopulations. For this reason, it can be dangerous for the practitioner to apply general Hispanic population data to the design of developmental strategies focused on one specific subgroup. General Hispanic data, however, are useful in identifying possible issues or factors that may be relevant to any particular Hispanic group.

The College Pool. Proportionately fewer Hispanics graduate from high school than do non-Hispanics. As of March 1982, for persons twenty-five years or older, 46 percent of Hispanics were high school graduates, compared to 72 percent of the Anglo population (U.S. Department of Commerce, 1985). Although the Hispanic population is growing, Hispanics will continue to be underrepresented in U.S. college enrollment statistics because of the smaller pool of Hispanic candidates for college, their lower median incomes, and the scarcity of funding. These data suggest that current cutbacks in recruitment and retention programs that are specifically designed for Hispanic students are most untimely and not in keeping with a commitment to higher Hispanic enrollment rates.

Part-Time Enrollment. In 1978, 42 percent of Hispanic students, compared to 23 percent of non-Hispanic students, were enrolled either full- or part-time in two-year colleges. There is a greater part-time to full-time enrollment ratio among Hispanics, as compared to non-Hispanics (Durán, 1983). This fact has definite implications for practitioners in terms of program design and implementation. Career choices and marketability of skills for Hispanic professionals in the future are also affected.

Curricula. Proportionately fewer Hispanics were enrolled in business, science, or technology curricula, as compared to the non-Hispanic population (Durán, 1983). A historic Hispanic educational emphasis on arts and letters, as opposed to the empirical disciplines, may explain this phenomenon; however, the absence of significant career counseling during the formative years also contributes to this disparity between liberal arts and the technical curricula.

Location Choice. Hispanics seem to enroll in schools in areas of high Hispanic population concentration, such as the Southwest for Mexican-Americans, major Eastern urban centers for Puerto Ricans, and southern Florida for Cubans. From March 1981 to March 1982, one in every five

Hispanics changed residence, but most of these moves occurred within very short distances. The majority of Hispanics remained in the same standard metropolitan statistical areas (U.S. Department of Commerce, 1985). This tendency limits college options for Hispanics and presents special challenges to institutions that are outside of these Hispanic population concentrations and that wish to enhance their general student-body profiles by admitting Hispanic students.

According to the Bureau of the Census, geographical mobility rate among Hispanics is directly related to inclusion in the labor force. Hispanics sixteen years or older who were active in the labor force had a higher geographical mobility rate than those who were not (U.S. Department of Commerce, 1985). This fact suggests that an eventual increase in career options for Hispanics, through increased access to higher educational opportunities, will facilitate percentage representations of Hispanics in geographical areas heretofore considered insignificant.

Role Models. It is a generally accepted premise that significant interaction with role models displaying a targeted characteristic will have a positive effect on the development of said characteristic in the individual. In general, Hispanics come from families whose heads of household are more likely not to have graduated from high school (U.S. Department of Commerce, 1985). One way of giving students more interactions with role models would be for colleges and universities to utilize their Hispanic alumni and currently enrolled students and bring them into contact with Hispanics in elementary schools. College-sponsored tutoring programs, big brother/sister programs, and career days are some ways of increasing these interactions.

The Cuban Hispanic

Cuban-origin Hispanics are quite different from the rest of the U.S. Hispanic population. This fact is attributable to the unique history of Cubans in the United States, who numbered approximately 34,000 in 1950.

In 1959, as a result of actions taken by the Cuban regime of Fidel Castro, many highly educated, middle-class Cubans emigrated to the United States. Cuban Americans—given their high educational levels, high economic status, and tendency to come more from European than from Indian or Negroid ethnic stock—adapted to and integrated with the U.S. social and economic structure at a quicker rate than other Hispanic populations. However, this adaptation rate does not suggest a faster rate of cultural assimilation. Cubans, like other U.S. Hispanic populations, have preserved and maintained their ethnic heritage effectively. In 1976, 90 percent of Cuban-origin college students came from non–English-speaking home environments, as compared to 84 percent of Puerto Rican and Mexican American college students (Durán, 1983). The recent wave of Cubans entering the United States, with the Mariel boatlift of May 1980, has injected a totally different socioeconomic profile in the Cuban American population. These latter arrivals come from both a lower economic level as well as from more ethnically diverse backgrounds. The effect of this new population on Cuban socioeconomic attainment patterns has yet to be studied thoroughly.

Recommendations

Institutional Policy. In order to ensure meaningful higher education experiences for our nation's Hispanic populations, American colleges and universities must reaffirm their commitment to attract and retain more Hispanic students. Empirically based plans of action, with timelines and measurable outcomes designed to meet the educational needs of the various U.S. Hispanic student populations, should be developed and implemented.

Institutional policy statements should address such issues as developing institutional cultural awareness and sensitivity through staff development programs. Policies should include definite statements regarding the relationship between the institution and the Hispanic community, specific admissions criteria to be used for identifying qualified Hispanic students, and guidelines for and commitment to the hiring and promoting of Hispanic professionals. Administrative and academic departments responsible for implementing various institutional policies should be identified. Information on such policies, as well as information on the current status of their implementation, should be made available to the general public.

Colleges and universities should recognize that they cannot and should not operate in a vacuum with respect to members of the general Hispanic community. Input from concerned community sources should be solicited. Formal advisory groups and committees—consisting of individuals representing as many sectors of the local Hispanic community as possible, as well as of Hispanic undergraduate and graduate students and alumni members—should be established and actively used.

Staffing and Staff Development. Currently, many student affairs professionals without the necessary training and experience are assigned to work in areas of Hispanic student development. The ethics of such a practice are questionable. At best, it can be characterized as naively counterproductive; at worst, as a not particularly subtle sabotage of a weak commitment. True commitment to an effective program of recruitment and retention requires definite, basic measures of professional competence. Ongoing staff development programs need to be produced on such topics as Hispanic cultural awareness and appreciation, Hispanic student development theory, and Hispanic research and counseling methodologies. These staff development programs should include apprenticeship with experienced professionals, with certification in Hispanic student development as a possible goal. Ongoing staff development offerings required for maintenance of certification could also be provided.

Professional staff should become involved with Hispanic students as often as possible, and annual faculty evaluations should include assessment of the quality of such involvement. All staff should become aware that competency in working with Hispanic students will be considered in awards of merit raises and promotions.

Colleges and universities need to recruit, hire, and promote more Hispanic professionals in all areas, including student affairs, teaching, and administration. A concentration of Hispanics in strictly minority-related positions defeats the philosophy of equal access to all areas of the campus. This narrowly focused hiring process conveys a negative message about institutional receptivity to Hispanics, and this negativity may affect Hispanics' willingness to enroll in particular institutions.

Liaisons with the Private Sector. Traditionally, institutions have been reluctant to involve the private sector significantly in the educational process. In contrast, as beneficiaries of the end product of the formal education process—a well-educated employee—corporations have recognized the need to establish and maintain communication with the educational community. As the Hispanic national consumer market continues to increase at astonishing rates, industries need professionals in all disciplines who can contribute to the development of this market. Corporate foundations should be pursued as sources of funding and of political support for scholarships, programs, and services geared toward developing Hispanic talent. To accomplish this goal, university administrators must develop keen awareness of and respect for corporate cultures.

Admissions. If colleges are to attract successful Hispanic students, admissions decisions must be based on a broader set of factors than achievement test scores and grade point averages. Two obvious necessities are research to determine college success predictors and measurements that can be more realistically applied to the various Hispanic student populations.

As suggested earlier, preadmission programs administered to students should be initiated as early as junior high school. These programs should be designed to meet the special informational needs of Hispanic parents and siblings. This goal can be achieved through increased interactions and open communication between college and secondary school educators and administrators and through the creation of institutional policies that value positive relations with the Hispanic community in general.

Orientation Programs. Special attention should be given to the quality of Hispanic students' initial college experiences. Substantial orientation experiences should be designed that actually meet the needs of Hispanic students and their parents and that follow parents and students beyond matriculation and the first week of class.

Hispanic orientation activities—emphasizing such skills as learning to study, taking notes and tests, establishing personal finances, developing interpersonal relationships, seeking values clarification, practicing assertiveness, and engaging in academic planning and career exploration—should be offered for credit to provide cultural college-orientation learning experiences.

Summary

Although the fact that Hispanics may become the largest minority group in the United States by the year 1990 has been highly publicized, socioeconomic conditions may prohibit a corresponding growth in the Hispanic college population unless proactive measures are taken. American higher education must accept the challenge of bringing economic and educational parity to Hispanic groups through effective recruitment and retention programs and practices.

This goal presents a special challenge to higher-education professionals. The relatively high numbers of Hispanics now in elementary school could mean increased numbers of Hispanics in college in the next ten years, if educators prepare for their admission into higher education by doing long-range planning. Colleges and universities need to become tomorrow-oriented. The profile of the future consumers of higher education will be drastically different from the profile today; and, even under less than optimum conditions, Hispanic students definitely will become an important population in the coming years.

The quality of the college experience for these students depends on the quality of the preparedness of the educational system. To reiterate, the necessary measures for colleges are:

- Programmatic interventions geared toward developing basic academic, assertiveness, and career-assessment skills during the Hispanic's precollege years
- Involvement of the family as much as possible in the early admission, orientation, and follow-up counseling processes
- Creative funding strategies for Hispanic-oriented programs that involve the private sector, and reaffirmation of commitment to the recruitment and retention of Hispanic college students at the institutional level
- More programmatic focus on the needs of individual Hispanic populations, as opposed to design of programs that falsely assume homogeneity among Hispanic students
- Longitudinal research into the various factors that positively affect Hispanic academic achievement
- Sincere efforts to involve Hispanic educators, students, and the community at large in administrative decision-making processes that directly affect Hispanics.

63

References

Astin, A. W. *Minorities in American Higher Education: Recent Trends, Current Prospects, and Recommendations.* San Francisco: Jossey-Bass, 1982.

Beal, P. E., and Noel, L. *What Works in Student Retention.* Iowa City, Iowa: American College Testing Program and the National Center for Higher Education Management Systems, 1984.

Berry, J. W. "Acculturation as Varieties of Adaptation." In A. A. Padilla (ed.), *Acculturation: Theory, Models and Some New Findings.* Boulder, Colo.: Westview Press, 1980.

Chickering, A. W. *Education and Identity.* San Francisco: Jossey-Bass, 1969.

Durán, R. P. *Hispanics' Education and Background: Predictors of College Achievement.* New York: College Entrance Examination Board, 1983.

Ford Foundation. *Hispanics: Challenges and Opportunities.* Working paper #435. New York: Ford Foundation, 1984.

Grossman, H. *Educating Hispanic Students.* Springfield, Ill.: Thomas, 1984.

Herring, H. *A History of Latin America.* New York: Random House, 1967.

Naisbitt, J. *Megatrends.* New York: Warner Books, 1984.

Schreiner, T. "Poverty Worsens for Hispanic Americans." *The San Francisco Chronicle,* September 3, 1986, p. 10.

U.S. Department of Commerce, Bureau of the Census. *Persons of Spanish Origin in the United States: March 1982.* Current Population Reports. *Population Characteristics.* Series P-20, no. 396. Washington, D.C.: U.S. Government Printing Office, 1985.

Wolf, E. *Sons of the Shaking Earth.* Chicago: University of Chicago Press, 1972.

Ennio L. Quevedo-García is managing director of Inroads–San Francisco Bay, Incorporated, an educational nonprofit corporation. He has formerly held campus activities and orientation positions at the University of Texas at Austin and the University of Nebraska at Lincoln.

American Indians do not strive to assimilate into the white culture. Higher education must recognize Indian college students' perspective to effectively meet their needs.

American Indian Students in College

Deborah Wetsit LaCounte

Historical Background of American Indian Education

Commitment to education for American Indians on the part of the people of the United States dates back to the early development of this country's education system. In 1723, William and Mary College opened special facilities to house the Indian students who were enrolled. The Continental Congress approved $500 in 1775 for the education of Indians at Dartmouth College. Many of the treaties negotiated by the federal government with American Indian tribes included specific provisions for the education of Indian children.

The Snyder Act of 1921 authorized the Bureau of Indian Affairs to provide educational services to American Indians. The Bureau of Indian Affairs assumed primary responsibility for higher education assistance granted to Indian students who met their criteria of having one-fourth Indian blood and being enrolled in a federally recognized tribe.

The Indian Reorganization Act (Wheeler-Howard Bill) of 1934 established the powers of tribal governments, enabling tribes to be self-governing entities. The policy represented a major shift by the United States government from trying to eliminate the land base and destroy the culture of the tribes to strengthening and enlarging tribal governing pow-

D. J. Wright (ed.). *Responding to the Needs of Today's Minority Students.*
New Directions for Student Services, no. 38. San Francisco: Jossey-Bass, Summer 1987.

ers. The Act included a provision for vocational education for Indian people and specifically authorized loans to pay for tuition and other expenses in postsecondary educational programs.

As the number of Indian college students increased and resources allocated to this budget item became strained, alternatives available to low-income students were considered. Havighurst (1981) reported that after 1960, proportions of Indian youth began to attend postsecondary institutions. This proportion probably multiplied fivefold between 1960 and 1970. Approximately 8,000 Indian students, about 12 percent aged eighteen to twenty-one years, were in universities or postsecondary colleges in 1970. Further, Havighurst revealed that 3,432 Bureau of Indian Affairs scholarships were awarded in 1969, with an average of $868 per student, as compared to 15,000 Bureau of Indian Affairs scholarships awarded in 1975, with an average of $1,750. About 1976, the Bureau of Indian Affairs began viewing its grant funds for higher education as supplementary, rather than as a primary resource, which caused its role in higher education to change dramatically.

In 1985, 919 scholarships were awarded in the Billings (Montana) Bureau of Indian Affairs office alone, with an average grant award of $1,891. While the total amount of the Bureau of Indian Affairs' contribution has not increased significantly, other resources available to the student are not reflected in this figure. The Indian college student had only to work with the Bureau of Indian Affairs education specialist to complete the necessary applications and verification of eligibility in order to attend college.

Profile of American Indian Students in Higher Education

The cultural diversity among American Indian tribes becomes quickly evident to the beginning scholar of Indian affairs. In the United States alone, over 481 Indian tribes are recognized by the federal government (League of Women Voters Education Fund, 1976). Another 17 tribes are recognized by state governments, and 52 other tribal entities are not recognized by either level of government (Locke, 1978). In the state of Montana, for example, there are seven Indian reservations with a total of 10 tribal groups: Assiniboine, Blackfeet, Chippewa, Cree, Crow, Gros Ventre, Kootenai, Northern Cheyenne, Salish, and Sioux. Each tribe has language differences and custom variations but enough commonalities to refer to the groups as "Plains Indian culture." It is not unusual to find each of these tribal groups represented at all Montana colleges.

Enrollment in college is frequently the first long-term exposure to a non-Indian environment for Indian students, many of whom attended high school on reservations, where Indian enrollment ranges up to 98 percent. Because Indian reservations are generally in rural areas and foster different cultures from those typically found on college campuses, a substantial impact is felt by the matriculating Indian student. Only a tremendous desire for learning and personal growth propels the student into so foreign and uncomfortable an environment; only great effort by both student and institution makes retention possible.

College adjustment programs, such as Eastern Montana College's Indian Career Services Program, are essential to the American Indian college (Falk and Aitken, 1984; Wright, 1985; Maynard, 1980). Brown found that "adjustment programs are deemed necessary because traditional support programs available to all students are usually underutilized by Indians" (Brown, 1981, p. 117).

Most student affairs professionals are alert to the diversity of minority populations and to the culture shock they experience to greater or lesser degrees upon matriculation. However, there is another factor at work, about which they are too often uninformed and insensitive. Perhaps Nieves (1978, p. 10) said it best: "Essentially, when there exist expectations (stereotypes) of one group from another, a form of culture shock results. Many college administrators are amazed that minority students do not appear to be grateful. They feel that minority students are not 'really entitled or qualified' and, therefore, should express gratitude for the opportunity to be in college. Many minority students, in contrast, accurately view their admission as an earned right and are conscious that they bring something rich and valuable to the college."

Lack of Academic Preparation

Reservation high schools have steadily improved since the 1970s. Indian people are involved as board members, teachers, and administrators, but the isolated environment still presents obstacles that have not been conquered. The Indian student enters college less well prepared academically than her or his non-Indian counterpart. Astin (1982), acknowledging sparse data, indicated that 45 percent of Indian students leave the educational system before graduating from high school. Coladarci (1983) estimated a 60 percent dropout rate among Indian students in several Montana high schools where Indians constituted about 90 percent of the student body. Astin's (1975) earlier study found that the most dropout-prone freshmen were those with poor high school academic records, low aspirations, poor study habits, relatively uneducated parents, and small-town backgrounds. These students were also older than most other freshmen. When one considers that many Indian college students fall into all or most of these categories, it is amazing that any have graduated at all.

If we assume that the student profile at Eastern Montana College is typical of Indian students at similar institutions, then we find the following data. Approximately 95 percent of Indian students receive some type of financial aid; about 46 percent are of nontraditional college age, over twenty-five; 51 percent or more are married or single parents; 21 percent live on campus in the dorms; 22 percent commute from beyond a thirty-mile radius; 57 percent live in the college town; and a large number of freshmen require remedial courses in math and English. These figures indicate a predominately low-income, older Indian student body, the majority of whom have families and either live in the college town or commute from nearby reservations.

Variables That Influence College Persistence

Several variables—including financial resources, bilingualism, and career awareness—are believed to affect an Indian student's college persistence. Few Indian students begin college with resources other than what they receive through financial aid. High levels of unemployment on the reservations severely limit students' ability to save money for education and families' ability to serve as a monetary resource during the school year.

Bilingualism varies according to tribe. Crow students who attended Eastern Montana College have a very high bilingual ability, nearly 80 percent, while other tribes have fewer native-language speakers (Schindler and Davidson, 1985). Students' identification with other Indian students varies from having no desire to associate with other Indians to wanting to associate with other Indians exclusively; the majority fall somewhere between these extremes.

Indian high school students aspire to occupations visible on or near the reservations in which they live (Hurlburt, Schulz, and Eide, 1985). This fact restricts their ability to consider different career options. Lack of career awareness and direction is frequently evident at the college level. A common remark among incoming Indian students is that they want to earn a degree and go back to the reservation and help their people. This concern for helping their people and the expectation that a college degree will provide greater employment possibilities and financial security are the strongest motivators of the Indian student and may outweigh the negative impact of limited career awareness.

Recruitment Strategies

One of the most important characteristics of the college recruiter of Indian students is identification with the Indian community. Indian communities lack trust in the system and in those representing the system, and there is a strong emphasis on personal contact within the culture. Therefore, it is essential that recruiters visit the reservation communities and personally talk to potential students, parents, tribal leaders, and educators. These visits should be made annually. Indian students can also play a formal role in the recruiting effort, either by accompanying recruiters or by representing the college individually.

The establishment of special programs addressing the specific needs of the Indian student is also a valuable recruiting tool. The Eastern Montana College Math/Science/PreEngineering/Medical Professionals Program for American Indian students, the University of New Mexico's Native American/College of Engineering Program, and the University of North Dakota's In-Med Program are strong statements to the incoming Indian student that the college is sensitive to Indian students' culture and needs, and here exist support, concern, and interest.

Recruitment should not be limited to high school seniors or graduates. Astin (1982) found that among high school graduates, the minority group least likely to go directly to college was American Indians: Only about 27 percent enroll immediately after high school graduation, as compared to 45–47 percent for white students. Recruitment efforts should reach out to older high school alumni and should always include the potential student's family, who, in the Indian culture, is very influential in the decision-making process.

Interventions That Enhance Academic and Personal Development

Orientation. Most colleges conduct orientation programs designed to facilitate students' successful integration into unfamiliar and social settings (Pascarella, Terenzini, and Wolfe, 1986). In addition to the campus tour, orientation programs generally provide an overview of administrative policies and procedures, available student services, campus organizations, and academic advising. Indian students generally do not attend such orientation sessions.

A recent study revealed that students who chose to attend orientations were white, more socially integrated, and from higher socioeconomic levels. They also had higher levels of commitment to the college than did Indian or other minority students (Pascarella, Terenzini, and Wolfe, 1986). A program such as the Eastern Montana College Math/Science/PreEngineering/Medical Professionals Program is especially designed for subsets of the Indian student population. This orientation program not only includes the campus tour for the student and his or her significant others (who are strongly urged to attend) but also extends an invitation to faculty members to address students on particular subjects, such as career options and study skills. Indian students in particular need the opportunity to meet members of the faculty on an informal basis. Such meetings are a first step toward encouraging students to see the faculty as nonthreatening individuals who care and want to see each student succeed. Indian students do not automatically view their instructors in this context. To them, the faculty and staff may represent the system, and the Indian does not trust the system.

Another possible variation of the orientation session has been initiated at Eastern Montana College. A special orientation class is conducted daily for two weeks at the beginning of the fall quarter. The class addresses all that is typically found in orientation sessions, but in greater depth. "Should I talk to my professor if I did not get an assignment?" "I don't know how to take notes; what do I do?" "I missed class; now what?" These questions and more are answered, to the benefit of all the students.

Specialized summer programs, such as the Headlands Indian Health Career Programs at the University of Oklahoma (Hardy, 1986) and the Math, Engineering, and Science Achievement Program of the University of New Mexico, bring Indian high school students on campus for six to eight weeks for course work and enrichment activities (Cummings, 1984). College student support programs should provide assistance to the organizers of such efforts as frequently as possible to ensure early contact with high school students.

Institutional Retention Efforts. Student affairs programs for American Indian students require a high level of personal contact and follow-up. Various counseling services are needed in admissions, adjustment to college life, financial aid, career, employment, and personal and health care. This type of program may provide general education advising as well as referral services to appropriate departments when students declare majors.

Admittedly, this is a wide range of responsibility for any office to undertake, but it is necessary. It is crucial that the staff of such programs be knowledgeable about the resources available at college, community, and reservation levels to allow effective referrals. The goal of assisting the whole person, and not just meeting specific needs, is a basic premise of the American Indian culture.

A major role for the staff members of an Indian student service program is to provide support. This can be accomplished through motivational talks, a caring attitude, and advocacy. At the end of each quarter or semester, letters of support for good grades and letters of concern for poor grades let the students know they are important and that someone cares.

Many of the students' concerns are of an immediate nature. Evans (1977) emphasized that the key word for counselors of Indian students is *accessibility*, which cannot be overemphasized. Requiring students to make appointments is certainly a convenience to the counselor, but it is ineffective for addressing immediate concerns. Whenever possible, staff should be available to talk with students on request, even though these demands on limited staff time will require extra effort and careful scheduling.

Academic and Career Advising. A student's basic skills should be adequately assessed at the beginning of his or her academic career; for an Indian student, this is especially important. An academic adviser should never make global assumptions about Indian students' backgrounds. In the absence of testing data, discussions about high school background and types of classes taken and clear descriptions of entry-level expectations of college courses will help determine which classes are appropriate.

Although all college students ideally should have the basic high school preparation necessary for earning a college degree, this is not always the case. Montana maintains an open-admissions system. All state residents who have earned a high school diploma from a fully accredited high school or who have earned a G. E. D. are accepted at state-supported institutions. Open admissions introduce the question of who is responsible for the educational needs, and specifically the remedial needs, of the students once they are admitted to college. At colleges with admissions requirements, Evans (1977) strongly advises, personal interviews should be a high priority for Indian students to ensure that Indian students with potential for college success are admitted.

Brown (1981) recommended encouraging students to delay selection of majors until completion of the freshman year. This strategy keeps students' options open and encourages further career exploration. Job opportunities and greater job security are concerns that motivate many Indian students, but lack of career awareness, due to the rural reservation environment, definitely limits the career options they consider on their own. Career awareness classes or workshops addressing the rural Indian reservation environment are essential; they should also address job-search skills, such as employment applications, résumés, interviewing, nonverbal communication, and employer expectations. Internships offer another type of valuable career experience. Staff can suggest internships and assist students in securing effective placement. Work-study positions in various professional settings offer additional career exposure that many students from the reservation otherwise may not receive.

A very effective means of gaining students' attention regarding career options is the use of Indian professionals as role models and as proof that it is possible to become a lawyer, engineer, social worker, educator, and so forth. Eastern Montana Indian Career Services has found Indian professionals very willing to share their time and talk to students, both formally and informally. This strategy has been recommended by various sources and has proved effective in programs at Eastern Montana College and at the University of New Mexico (Astin, 1982; Wright, 1985; Lujan and Hill, 1981; Maynard, 1980).

Monitoring Academic Progress. Programs that closely monitor students' academic progress run the risk of appearing paternalistic and untrusting of the student. This danger is real, and the determination of the need for such action must be thought through carefully. One of the mildest forms of staff intervention is to rely on faculty requests, which can involve the faculty member's concerns regarding high absenteeism, a failed test, or a general request to offer additional encouragement. An effort is made by Indian Career Services to let faculty know that the staff is available to follow up on any concerns they want to bring to the staff's attention. This approach depends on sensitive faculty and is very effective.

A second approach is to secure grade lists of all Indian students after each quarter or semester, noting grade point averages, types of classes, and number of credits completed. Students who appear to be having difficulty are invited by letter to come in and talk with a counselor. This approach allows the student to decide if intervention is needed. Counselors may want to initiate contact. This approach reaches more students than either of the above two methods and requires initiative from staff as well as students.

The third approach is used in the Eastern Montana State College Math/Science/PreEngineering/Medical Professionals Program. The staff contacts faculty members on a regular basis throughout the quarter and requests academic progress reports on students involved with this program. Students are aware that faculty will be contacted. The staff also maintains daily contact with students, who generally provide realistic evaluations of their progress. Brigham Young University instructs faculty members to report excessive absences, poor tests scores, and homework delinquency to the advisement center, which then contacts students to offer appropriate assistance (Osborne and Cranney, 1985). Again, the staff's efforts can be misinterpreted, and so open communication with students is paramount.

Tutorial Support. Otis (1981) notes that tutorial services are important in retaining Indian students in college. Lack of academic preparation prior to college enrollment makes it reasonable to expect a high need for tutoring. Many of the programs described in the literature for Indian students refer to a tutoring component (Osborne and Cranney, 1985; Cummings, 1984; Illinois State Board of Education, 1983; Whiteman, 1978). A strong message must be sent to the students needing assistance, telling them that it is acceptable to seek tutoring. Indian students should also be encouraged to serve as tutors. Colleges can borrow from the University of New Mexico's Math, Engineering, and Science Achievement Program for high school students, which employs advanced students to provide tutorial support for freshmen, as well as using professional engineers and scientists (Cummings, 1984).

Financial Aid. The financial aid system has spawned a massive amount of paperwork, making it essential that American Indian student affairs staff be knowledgeable about institutional policies and practices. Older students still remember when potential college students merely contacted the Bureau of Indian Affairs education specialist before registering for college classes; this is no longer possible. Indian students now must work with the college financial aid office, meet all its criteria, and complete all its forms and verification requirements, in addition to those required by the Bureau of Indian Affairs. The amount of paperwork involved is astonishing, not to mention frustrating. Students must make certain that all forms have been received by appropriate agencies and are being processed without problems. It is especially confusing for students to determine how much aid they will be receiving, since the campus financial aid office must coordinate with all other available resources in determining a total financial aid package, and this does take time. When a problem develops, the student must determine whom to contact.

The basic types of financial aid do not cover all the typical student's expenses, especially with the current expectation that each student will contribute to his or her own education. It is important to know what types of contributions acceptably meet this guideline. Indian college students need information about alternative resources, such as private foundations, scholarships, and special programs designed to assist minority students.

Thus, the campus financial aid office has a much greater impact on the Indian college student today, since the Bureau of Indian Affairs serves only as a supplemental source of funding. Moreover, the determination of budgetary needs is now in the hands of the college financial aid office, which is concerned with all students, not just with Indian students.

Unfortunately for all, the typical college student's budget frequently is not suited to the Indian student's situation. For example, the College Scholarship Service computation procedures, followed by the many colleges who subscribe to their services, recommend the amount students are expected to contribute toward their education-related expenses. The current recommendation stipulates that each independent student is expected to contribute $400 per quarter to college expenses (College Scholarship Service, 1986). This contribution can be made through a well-paying summer job or through part-time employment during the academic year. All things being equal, this plan makes good sense; but all things are not equal. Unemployment on Indian reservations is very high, as high as 90 percent. The same cultural factors that hinder adjustment to a college environment and to living off the reservation also apply when students consider seeking employment from predominantly non-Indian employers. These factors severely limit the possibility that Indian students will find employment in a college town. The result is that the financial aid office shows that the Indian student has no unmet financial need, and that all expenses are covered by resources available, because the expected earned income is written into the student's budget as a resource, regardless of whether it exists or not, and the Indian student survives, if at all, by doing with even less.

The area of personal finances is a major battleground for basic value conflicts between the traditional Indian culture and the non-Indian culture. The value conflict begins when family members visit and the

Indian student is not budgeted to feed or entertain visitors, or when there is a ceremony that requires the student's attendance but the budget does not allow for extra trips home, or when a family members needs financial help and the student is the only one with any resources, but the budget does not allow for helping anyone.

Indian students frequently face this type of tug-of-war between what they know the financial aid office says are necessities and what their reality dictates to be necessities (Zitzow and Estes, 1981). Again, the student does without necessities. When the student is presented with the budgetary figures and the rationale behind each figure, the student agrees that adequate finances are necessary. To highlight this fact is not to downplay the need to develop the budgeting skills that many college students lack, but rather simply to illustrate that there is a value conflict here. In many cases, Indian students' actual needs go unrecognized.

For the highest retention rates, financial aid offices would ideally (1) acknowledge that an Indian student having difficulty adjusting to the college environment cannot reasonably be expected to contribute through employment until adjustment to college takes place and (2) allow flexibility in the student's budget to meet unexpected needs. No one can predict when she or he will find it necessary to meet cultural obligations beyond the scope of the budget, especially over a four- or five-year academic period. Brown (1981) proposes a system to allocate a basic amount to each student for secondary costs, such as those that exceed the costs of tuition, room and board (residence halls), and books, thus allowing students to decide which secondary costs will have priority. This idea is potentially very effective for addressing culturally related concerns if all secondary costs are taken into consideration.

The Bureau of Indian Affairs also needs to review its responsibilities to the American Indian college student. The cost of moving to a college community are virtually ignored. Students are left to whatever means they can find to secure moving expenses. If the only means of moving is through borrowing, then that debt will contribute to future financial difficulties.

Indian people have a high level of mistrust of non-Indian officials. Research by LaFramboise and Dixon (1981) found that the Indian person is likely to enter a situation not trusting until trustworthiness is proved, as compared to the non-Indian attitude of trusting until trust is broken. This dilemma is one faced frequently by the financial aid office and by the vast majority of Indian students who come in contact with this office. Indian personnel should be employed here. Students and students' significant others—spouses, parents, aunts, grandmothers, and so forth—approach Indian Career Services frequently to confirm that financial aid personnel are telling them all that they should know or to ask for clarification of the information provided. At work here is the Indian student's mistrust of the system represented by this office; in no way is it a reflection of the trustworthiness of financial aid employees.

Peer Counseling. An important resource available to incoming college students is the established student body. Indian students at the junior and senior levels know the campus, the instructors, and the formal "ins and outs" of campus life, and their knowledge can provide valuable assistance to new and transfer students.

Eastern Montana College has recently implemented a student advocate group to draw on this resource. Each upper-division student is asked to serve as a contact and support person for up to five entering students. A brief orientation is conducted, and intermittent contact is maintained. Several activities are planned by the upper-division students, such as game night, pizza night, and movies. Montana State University has a similar peer counseling program.

Student Organizations. The most common type of campus-based organization in which students participate is the Indian Club. This organization is a valuable resource for Indian students, allowing and encouraging them to organize student activities that lend the richness of the Indian culture to the college campus and give each other support in the college environment. Many of these clubs date from the late Sixties and the early Seventies, such as the Eastern Montana College Inter-Tribal Indian Club and the University of Montana's Kyi Yo Indian Club.

The Indian Club plays a major role in retaining new students by enabling students to establish contact with each other. Another type of Indian Club has evolved recently via the American Indian Science and Engineering Program student chapters. These chapters are more specialized in that they address the needs and interests of students involved in the math, science, and engineering disciplines—definitely an exciting variation.

While an Indian Club provides a base of common ground and interest for Indian college students, they should also be encouraged to join other campus organizations, such as student government, clubs in their major areas, and community-related efforts. Tinto (1975), in his discussion of extracurricular involvement for college students in general, indicated that such activities provide a major link to the social and academic systems of the college and may help reduce the strain between the demands of the two systems.

Cultural Events. A major event on Montana's campuses is the annual pow wow. The pow wow consists of intertribal dancing, specialty dances, feasts, and honoring ceremonies. Ths event permits students to honor and recognize individuals in the "home away from home" college environment. The beauty of such occasions is that the college campus is transformed into an environment that is fully accepting of the Indian people. Grandmothers and grandfathers of students can stroll the campus that their grandchildren travel seeking knowledge. Indian students proudly offer a glimpse of their culture for the enjoyment and learning of their non-Indian colleagues. Strong feelings of cultural pride and camaraderie prevail among the Indian students during and after a successful pow wow. Sponsoring such events speaks highly of the institution's sensitivity and support of the American Indian culture.

Future Directions for Support Programs

The age of technology moves quickly. The dominant culture places high regard on change, on acquiring the latest products, and on learning the newest methods and discarding the old. Culture for U.S. society seems to exist today, if not tomorrow. Culture for the American Indian people, while acknowledging the inevitability of change, is still based on the traditions of the past. It is not the goal of Indian people to assimilate into the dominant culture but to retain their own uniqueness, their own identity. It is important to note this difference because there is a widening of the gap between the two cultures in many ways, as one culture strains to move into the future and the other relies heavily on the ways of the elders.

American Indian student affairs programs must provide the necessary support to assist Indian students in dealing with this difference. Zitzow and Estes (1981) provide a heritage-consistency continuum to help counselors recognize some of the factors involved. Indian people must develop two identities—one that is at home looking up at the sky through the poles of the medicine lodge, and one that is comfortable in a business suit in a conference room.

Institutions must recognize that more than one culture exists and has value. McDonald (1978) expressed his opinion that institutions must learn to accept other values and other meaningful life objectives before Indian college students will stop dropping out. This is a challenging situation at best, and the time has come for adaptation.

Funding Stability. It seems that Indian support programs must always justify their existence, especially in times of financial exigency or proposed structural change. American Indian programs seem to be on the fringe when it comes to long-range planning, even though most changes affect their programs and the wide range of services they provide. American Indian student affairs programs exist to address the needs of a specific minority population. It takes a relatively stable future outlook to promote the growth and development of such programs.

Tribally Controlled Community Colleges. There are eighteen tribally controlled community colleges in the United States, not including the three Bureau of Indian Affairs postsecondary institutions. The role that the tribally controlled community colleges play on the reservation is significant as enrollment increases; however, a much stronger liaison is needed between these colleges and four-year institutions, perhaps even an exchange of faculty and jointly sponsored faculty/staff development training. Open communication between student affairs divisions is a necessity to ensure that students' needs are being met at both institutions. If the tribes want their members to begin at the tribally controlled community colleges and to continue at the four-year institutions, then close coordination between the institutions is particularly important, given studies showing that few community college students actually complete four-year college degrees (Astin, 1975; Cope, 1978).

Communication Successes. Student affairs programs exist to support students' efforts and to promote their development. Students must know that someone cares whether they are doing well in class. It is very important that counselors reach out to American Indian students and not wait until they make appointments, especially for follow up. It is important to recognize and effectively use Indian communication patterns that have evolved from Indian culture and are evident in the effective counseling of Indian students. While confidentiality is essential to all counseling, its importance in counseling the American Indian cannot be overemphasized.

Minority students' voices and triumphs can be lost in the largeness of the overall student body. It is important that this not be permitted to happen. American Indian student affairs programs can ensure that the positive contributions and successes of the Indian student body receive due recognition. Students' successes can be highlighted in the campus newspaper, as well as local and tribal newspapers. Promotion of a high student profile in the community can be accomplished by encouraging students to get involved in community benefit projects.

Student affairs personnel will find themselves serving as student advocates with other staff and members of the faculty. They should not assume that because there is awareness of Indian students on campus there is also sensitivity. American Indian student affairs staff have a major role in educating the student population with whom they work.

In the late Sixties and the early Seventies, Indian leaders contributed their ideas and opinions to a variety of journals and other publications. Indian leaders today seem to be involved with the practical application of what appear to be effective practices, but few are now writing about their efforts for the benefit of other professionals. There is a definite need for more reporting and research in all areas of American Indian student services, such as culturally relevant career-interest inventories and maturity measurements, effective counseling techniques, and so on.

Staff of American Indian programs are responsible for providing leadership and for serving as examples to students. Leadership encompasses a wide range of activities, such as participation in service projects within the college community, the local community, and the tribal community. Appropriate and sensitive professional behavior at all times is essential. Professionals in Indian support programs also should seek challenges outside these population-specific areas and become involved in related student affairs programs. These activities will broaden the support system and allow more American Indians into the system.

Summary

American Indian people do not strive for assimilation into the dominant society but want to keep their unique cultural identity. Higher education must recognize Indian college students' perspective to effectively meet their needs. Many successful programs exist that can serve as models for other colleges. The second-generation Indian college student is beginning to arrive on college campuses, showing that higher education is within reach through family role models and family support and understanding of Indian students' decisions to attend college. This in itself will result in change. It is hoped that this change can occur without the loss of a strong cultural identity.

References

Astin, A. W. *Preventing Students from Dropping Out*. San Francisco: Jossey-Bass, 1975.

Astin, A. W. *Minorities in American Higher Education: Recent Trends, Current Prospects, and Recommendations*. San Francisco: Jossey-Bass, 1982.

Brown, A. D. "Adjustment Programs for the American Indian College Student." In *Contemporary American Indian Issues in Higher Education*. Los Angeles: University of California, American Indian Studies Center, 1981.

Coladarci, T. "High School Dropout Among Native Americans." *Journal of American Indian Education*, 1983, *23* (1), 15–22.

College Scholarship Service. *CSS Need Analysis: Theory and Computation Procedures for the 1986–1987 FAF*. New York: The College Board, 1986.

Cope, R. G. "Why Students Stay, Why They Leave." In L. Noel (ed.), *Reducing the Dropout Rate*. New Directions for Student Services, no. 3. San Francisco: Jossey-Bass, 1978.

Cummings, T. *The Report of Engineering Special Programs, July 1, 1983–June 30, 1984*. 1984. (ED 251 255)

Evans, W. H. *American Indian Student Counselor Handbook*. Spearfish, S.D.: Black Hills State College, 1977.

Falk, D. R., and Aitken, L. P. "Promoting Retention Among American Indian College Students." *Journal of American Indian Education*, 1984, *23* (2), 24–31.

Hardy, T. "Headlands Indian Health Careers Program." *Winds of Change*, 1986, *1* (2), 12, 15.

Havighurst, R. J. "Indian Education Accomplishments of the Last Decade." *Phi Delta Kappan*, 1981, *62*, 329–331.

Hurlburt, G., Schulz, W., and Eide, L. "Using the Self-Directed Search with American Indian High School Students." *Journal of American Indian Education*, 1985, *25* (1), 34–41.

Illinois State Board of Education. *The Institute for Native American Development Model 1979–1983*. Springfield, Ill.: Springfield Department of Adult, Vocational, and Technical Instruction, 1983. (ED 233 165)

LaFromboise, T. D., and Dixon, D. N. "American Indian Perception of Trustworthiness in a Counseling Interview." *Journal of Counseling Psychology,* 1981, *28* (2), 135–139.

League of Women Voters Education Fund Indian Country. Washington, D.C.: League of Women Voters Education Fund, 1976.

Locke, P. "An Ideal School System for American Indians—A Theoretical Construct." In T. Thompson (ed.), *The Schooling of Native America.* Washington, D.C.: American Association of Colleges for Teacher Education, 1978.

Lujan, P., and Hill, L. B. "Intercultural Communication as an Academic Haven for Native American Studies." *Contemporary American Indian Issues in Higher Education.* Los Angeles: University of California, American Indian Studies Center, 1981.

McDonald, A. L. "Why Do Indian Students Drop Out of College?" In T. Thompson (ed.), *The Schooling of Native America.* Washington, D.C.: American Association of Colleges for Teacher Education, 1978.

Maynard, M. "Can Universities Adapt to Ethnic Minority Students' Needs?" *Journal of College Student Personnel,* 1980, *21* (4), 398–401.

Nieves, L. *College Achievement Through Self-Help: A Planning & Guidance Manual for Minority Students.* Princeton, N.J.: Graduate Record Examination Board and the Office for Minority Education of Educational Testing Service, 1978.

Osborne, V. C., and Cranney, A. G. *Elements of Success in a University Program for Indian Students.* 1985. (ED 257 611)

Otis, M. "Native Americans in Higher Education: Rationale and Retention." *Contemporary American Indian Issues in Higher Education.* Los Angeles: University of California, American Indian Studies Center, 1981.

Pascarella, E. T., Terenzini, P. T., and Wolfe, L. M. "Orientation to College and Freshman Year Persistence/Withdrawal Decisions." *The Journal of Higher Education,* 1986, *57* (2), 155–175.

Schindler, D. E., and Davidson, D. M. "Language, Culture, and the Mathematics Concepts of American Indian Learners." *Journal of American Indian Education,* 1985, *24* (3), 27–34.

Tinto, V. "Dropout from Higher Education: A Theoretical Synthesis of Recent Research." *Review of Educational Research,* 1975, *45* (1), 89–125.

Whiteman, H. V. "Native American Studies, the University, and the Indian Student." In T. Thompson (ed.), *The Schooling of Native America.* Washington, D.C.: American Association of Colleges for Teacher Education, 1978.

Wright, B. "Programming Success: Special Student Services and the American Indian College Student." *Journal of American Indian Education,* 1985, *24* (1), 1–7.

Zitzow, D., and Estes, G. "The Heritage Consistency Continuum in Counseling Native American Students." *Contemporary American Indian Issues in Higher Education.* Los Angeles: University of California, American Indian Studies Center, 1981.

Deborah Wetsit LaCounte is the director of Indian Career Services at Eastern Montana College in Billings, Montana. She is of the Assiniboine and Klamath tribes and is enrolled in the Fort Belknap Reservation in Montana.

*Future success of minority students at predominantly white
colleges rests on the quality of their campus interactions with
white peers in all campus settings.*

Enhancing Minority-White
Peer Interactions

W. Terrell Jones

During the 1960s and the 1970s, ethnic minorities enrolled on college
campuses in large numbers. As a result, predominantly white institutions
had to learn new ways of relating to these students. They had to redefine
their services and curricula to respond to the minority students' learning
needs. Those early minority-white relations were frequently awkward and
uncertain, with neither minority nor white students fully aware of one
another's needs. Institutions were unsure of how to develop strategies for
promoting minority-white relations. Almost three decades later, however,
it is time to evaluate our progress. Have minority-white relations matured
or regressed, and in what direction will they proceed in the years to come?

This chapter discusses the past, present, and future conditions of
minority-white relations on predominantly white college campuses. From
this historical overview comes a rationale for promoting change in institutional strategies to improve interactions among white and minority students. Recommendations for future programs and services are outlined.

The Changing Student Population

Historically, predominantly white campuses have educated those
students who best conformed to or fitted into existing campus norms.

D. J. Wright (ed.). *Responding to the Needs of Today's Minority Students.*
New Directions for Student Services, no. 38. San Francisco: Jossey-Bass, Summer 1987.

Most institutions assumed that the average student was eighteen to twenty-two years old, middle-class, and probably male. Anyone who did not fit these criteria was either denied admission or admitted as a "special student." Often these "special students" were members of ethnic minority groups, which began to enroll in college in significant numbers during the 1960s.

As these "special students" enrolled more frequently on campuses, specially designed support and academic services were created to assist them in their campus adjustment. These special programs were outside the academic mainstream. As a result, campuses saw the creation of such programs as black studies, academic support services, women's centers, returning-student programs, and so forth. These special programs were believed to address social and academic support needs of minorities and certain other students. In the process of providing minority students with academic and personal support, they often restricted those students' access to other college resources by separating them from the mainstream of the student population.

Higher education during the 1960s and the 1970s saw increased social consciousness and rapid change, much of which was brought about by the inclusion of minority students, whose values, customs, and thinking styles were vastly different from those of white students. Unfortunately, many minorities were not readily accepted. Many white students who had never interacted with minorities felt uncertain and confused about communicating with minority students. Likewise, institutions were confused and uncertain about the best methods of educating these students whose values and customs varied so from those of other students. They were unable and sometimes unwilling to anticipate the numerous changes that would occur in student populations and societal values (Peterson and others, 1978).

Because of these differences in values, beliefs, and behaviors, interpersonal conflict frequently arose among minority and white students. White and largely male institutions were unprepared and untrained to respond adequately to minority students' needs and to the interpersonal conflicts that minorities' introduction onto campus created.

A few white students sought to involve themselves with minority students in several ways, with mixed success. Some whites were active in civil rights and others undertook protest activities. Still others attended minority student cultural or entertainment or athletic events. Most white students, however, had little involvement with or interest in minority student activities and did not contribute to minority student enrollment (Peterson and others, 1978).

Because institutions misunderstood their impact, minority students, in order to survive, were expected to adjust to and assimilate into the campus environment, without regard for any of their cultural or learning-style differences. In short, minority students were expected to integrate into the campus if they were to become successful students. For many blacks and other minority students, integration with or conformity to accepted patterns was perceived as a sellout, a loss of identity (Gibbs, 1977).

As the civil rights movement escalated, minority students sought to represent their identity on campus in numerous ways. To white students, faculty, and administrators, minority students' emphasis on issues ranging from the campus availability of black hair-care products to social issues was misunderstood and added to the confusion. Minority students' emphasis on their own cultural identity uncovered racial tension between minority and white students. It was not unusual to hear blacks and whites tossing racial barbs at each other, one accusing the other of racial insensitivity and bigotry. White students perceived their black peers as cliquish, holding black-only social events and having vastly different life-styles. White students complained about black students' loud music, their different study habits, and their unique cultural, academic, and social interests. Black students, in contrast, evaluated whites as being insincere, racist, and unwilling to accept other cultures (Peterson and others, 1978).

Unfortunately, these complaints are still heard and contribute to increased racial tensions and racial incidents today (Turner, 1985). A survey of 160 colleges and universities revealed an increased pattern of racial incidents (Beckman, 1984). Given the mixed attitudes toward enforcement of civil rights and affirmative action by the federal government, racial tensions may continue to increase unless institutions accept responsibility for finding healthy ways to manage the conflict and tension that occur between minority and white student groups.

Minorities in the 1990s will continue to face discrimination in higher education that will affect all institutions adversely. If minorities are to experience higher education fully, then changes in white and minority student attitudes must occur. White students must reassess their biased racial, gender, and social-class attitudes and alter their behaviors and beliefs. Minorities must learn to evaluate which college environments best support their development and take responsibility for helping to create those settings. How minority and white students facilitate positive interactions will influence higher education far into the future.

Training Student Affairs Professionals

A key ingredient in enhancing minority-white relations on campus is training student affairs professionals to recognize minority students' learning, social, and developmental needs. In addition, professionals must be able to translate their new awareness into high-quality programs. For these reasons, examining how professionals are trained has significance for improving and enhancing minority-white relations.

In 1986 the Council for the Advancement of Standards for Student Services/Student Development Programs (CAS) issued standards and guidelines for student affairs master's levels programs. CAS recommended that a high-quality master's-level program include one or more of the following three basic dimensions: student development emphasis, administrative emphasis, and counseling emphasis (pp. 106–109).

A more critical review of the CAS standards and guidelines for master's-level preparation revealed that while minority-group issues are included in the guidelines, they are noted as comprising the "minimal essential standards" expected of any student personnel/student development program. One could become understandably confused when reviewing the CAS standards and guidelines. Although minority student services are included as a major section of the CAS document, this section's importance for training professionals was mentioned minimally in the master's-level preparation recommendations.

The development of many minority students at predominantly white institutions takes a path different from that of their white peers. Often, minority students experience problems in making the transition to college because the college environment and those working within it do not understand them. A student affairs professional training model applied to minority students should emphasize the total campus environment. Sensitive student affairs professionals must understand that being responsive to the needs of minority students is not sufficient; for many students, perception of the campus environment as hostile precipitates some adjustment problems.

There are several training models that educate professionals working with minority students. For example, Pedersen (1981) developed a model using cross-cultural triads, each triad matching a client with a counselor (dissimilar background) and an anticounselor (similar background). Pedersen has used the model in several hundred workshops through the United States. Workshop participants have reported being able to understand and articulate problems better after the workshop.

Katz (1978) developed a model that addressed racism in white people. Her model trained whites to understand and better manage their own racism. Reports from workshops using the Katz model at Pennsylvania State University indicated that close to 85 percent of the 1,100 workshop participants reported positive attitude changes.

Banks (1981) reported that cross-cultural counseling involved a process of self-examination, training, and practice. This process may also apply to student affairs tasks. Student affairs professionals need to expand their knowledge and skills in cultural diversity in order to improve their effectiveness with minority individuals. Banks developed a model for use in counselor training, a model relevant to student affairs professionals.

Modifying Banks' model, effective cross-cultural student affairs professionals do the following: clarify their own values, behaviors, and attitudes; view a problem from students' perspectives; improve professional skills through training, self-examination, and behavior change; implement strategies to reduce students' racial prejudice; communicate effectively with different ethnic groups; and strive for increased personal awareness of cultural and personality influences on minority students.

Student affairs professionals, according to Banks (1981), should demonstrate cross-cultural competence if they are to work effectively, but not everyone has agreed that cross-cultural competence is essential for student affairs professionals. Margolis and Rungta (1986) argue that special population training for counselors may be counterproductive. Similarly, Wilzosh (1983) and Griscom (1979) believe that accentuating subgroup differences may cause more divisiveness than understanding between groups. Other criticisms include budget restraints and the marketability of graduates with cross-cultural skills. Whether cross-cultural competence is beneficial for the student affairs professional appears to require more systematic investigation to bring clarity and reason to this complex, emotion-laden issue.

In summary, it appears that graduate-level student personnel/student development training programs are not fully cognizant of minority students' needs. Although training programs have expressed a commitment to helping professionals and graduate students upgrade their skills, they have not kept up with the changing demands of minority students. Masters' and doctoral training programs must find new ways to enhance cross-cultural competencies. The models suggested may help practitioners develop improved programs and services and enhance their own professional skills.

Student Development Theory and Minority Students

Minority students in predominantly white institutions face special social and academic adjustment problems. For some students, the college experience may represent the first or most significant exposure to a racially integrated environment, and its impact influences attitudes after leaving college (Fleming, 1984). For this reason, it is important to understand how minority students develop in college.

Student development theories describe the process by which a student matures and develops in college. Current student development theories suggest that most students proceed through similar developmental stages as they progress through college, yet these theories seem to ignore the effects that racism may have on progression through those developmental stages.

One may argue that student development theories misunderstand the role of race in the overall development of college students. For example, June and Pringle reviewed the concept of race in the career development theories of Roe, Super, and Holland and concluded that minority status was not adequately considered in these theories. Roe, Super, and Holland took their own cultural backgrounds, personal interests, and conceptions of the world as a theoretical framework and gave little weight to other backgrounds and cultures (June and Pringle, 1977).

Student development theories make two mistakes regarding minorities. First, they err by omission, failing to consider the many environmental and internal factors related to race. Second, they accept stereotypical attitudes about the achievement and abilities of ethnic minorities. These theories ignore the variations in learning and development that minority students bring to college. In doing so, they overlook an important ingredient in the overall development of college students, that of cultural influence. Theories that misunderstand the effects of culture and race are of questionable value to understanding minorities' developmental process, for in reality, culture and race appear to have a profound effect on their development.

Until student development theories account for race and cultural factors accurately in their interpretations of growth and development, student affairs programs must take the initiative in supporting minority students in their personal development while removing racial and cultural bias from their campus environments.

Multiethnic Education

Borrowed from elementary and high school settings, multiethnic education seeks to provide students with cultural and ethnic educational alternatives while reducing cultural encapsulation, or the tendency to view the world from only one perspective. Multiethnic education has been recommended for use in colleges and universities because faculty and staff, academic curricula, programs, and services have not prepared students satisfactorily to accept and affirm human diversity with respect to race, class, gender, disability, and age.

Banks (1981) identified several guidelines for the use of multiethnic education in elementary and secondary school settings. If reframed, these guidelines also may assist student affairs practitioners in their service delivery.

1. Ethnic pluralism should be encouraged across the entire campus.

2. Campus policies should foster positive multiethnic interactions among students, faculty, and professional and clerical support staff.

3. Instructional materials should reflect differences in students' learning styles.

4. Student affairs programs and services should help minority students with their self-development.

5. Student affairs programs and services should help all students develop their decision-making, social, and political skills for entry into an ethnically diverse work world.

6. Student affairs programs and services should encourage development of values, attitudes, and behaviors that accept ethnic pluralism.

7. Campuses should provide opportunities for students to recognize the aesthetic accomplishments of minority groups.

8. Student affairs professionals should help their students achieve effective interpersonal and group interactions among campus ethnic groups.

9. Student affairs professionals should encourage students to appreciate the contributions of campus minority groups.

10. Student affairs professionals should utilize ethnic minority community resources to help students learn about local minority resources.

Presumably, the by-products of multiethnic education are increased racial sensitivity and awareness, improved interethnic group communication, and enhanced student and professional cross-cultural skills. These skills affect the entire campus community by improving students' overall education experience and improving the quality of services provided to all students.

Conflict Theory and Minority Students

Interpersonal conflicts between minority and white students are often due to confusion regarding the cultural context of communication. Understanding the cultural context of students' interactions may help student affairs professionals understand interpersonal conflicts and their social and political consequences. Conflicts among students of different cultural groups are predictable, natural phenomena and, as such, are important for institutions to manage.

Understanding conflicts between minority and white students begins by recognizing their components. Interpersonal transactions can be divided into three communication systems, which are believed to exist in cultural settings: high-, low-, and middle-context transactions (Ting-Toomy, 1985). *High-context situations* contain uniformly accepted, pre-programmed information and norms that are known to the receiver and observed in the setting. In colleges and univesities, this context is seen in formal classroom settings. In *low-context situations,* such as residence halls, information and norms must be transmitted in order to communicate what is not explicit within the context. While no cultural group can be characterized as having high-, low-, or middle-context transactions exclusively, one may generalize about cultural behaviors on the basis of context evaluation. In cultures perceived as low in context, individual orientation and overt communication are valued. Conversely, within cultures high in context, value is placed on group identity orientation and covert, or hidden, communication patterns.

For example, the United States is at the low-context, heterogeneous end of the communication continuum, while Vietnamese culture is at the high-context, homogeneous end. Inherent in this communication framework is the notion that heterogeneous cultures create more conflict situations than do homogeneous ones. Thus, a minority student's culture of origin—Vietnamese, Puerto Rican, American Indian, Black American, and so forth—is thought to interact with the culture of higher education, often revealing interpersonal and intrapersonal conflicts at the interface. As college populations become heterogeneous, one could predict an increase in interpersonal conflicts, according to conflict theory. A student's perception and management of a given situation determine whether the conflicts become destructive or productive.

Hocker and Wilmot (1985) believe conflict may be a highly desirable and productive function in relationships. Conflict is threatening only when there are no appropriate avenues through which to manage it. Elastic cultures, those that allow the open and direct expression of conflict and that adjust to changing norms, are not likely to be threatened by conflict because they have developed appropriate ways to manage it.

Understanding conflict theory helps promote minority students' development. An example of this growth can be seen in campus governance practices. Governance practices that emphasize administrative decision-making control tend to favor people who understand the system, hold power positions, and affect institutional planning, programming, and budgeting. Traditional governance practices appear to perpetuate the status quo; thus, students have rarely been involved with them, yet what better place is there for minority students to learn conflict resolution strategies and acquire decision-making skills, than by participating in the governance of the institution where they have so much invested? By working in governance, students will learn about the culture of higher education. Minority students should be encouraged to become involved in campus governance as an aid to their clearer understanding of cultural contexts and especially of higher-education culture contexts.

Applications and Recommendations

Student Discipline Systems. Of special concern to student affairs administrators is student discipline and its role in the development and growth of minority students. A student discipline system, to be effective, should change periodically to reflect societal, attitudinal, and behavioral changes. Unfortunately, student discipline systems have rarely shifted in accordance with societal changes. Their failure to change may contribute to students' misunderstanding of each other, especially when minority students are involved.

Student discipline systems are inadequate for evaluating minority students' behaviors. Often, these systems are biased. Disciplinary decisions that do not recognize cultural differences in attitudes, beliefs, and behaviors are counterproductive for the entire college community. For example, student discipline systems are often ineffective with referrals involving racial slurs. In such cases, some white students, faculty, and administrators seem to believe in the old childhood rhyme "Sticks and stones may break my bones, but names will never hurt me." Minority and white students alike view such racial insults as yet another example of the institution's inability to manage campus racism. A discipline system trying to stop racial slurs is not helped when one of its participants holds unhealthy racial attitudes and beliefs. For practitioners to impose a programmed sanction against a student who exhibits open, negative racial behaviors, without trying to correct those behaviors, is unacceptable because they shirk their social responsibility to the student. Practitioners who are involved in student discipline services should use conflict theory, in concert with student development theory, to develop appropriate discipline strategies that are racially sensitive and enhance rather than impede personal growth and development.

One strategy college discipline systems should utilize is mediation, a process of negotiation conducted by an impartial and neutral third party to help disputing persons reach a mutually acceptable resolution of issues (Moore, 1986). Mediators are concerned with fair exchange, durability of a settlement, and enforceability. They advocate and become concerned with a fair process and not with a particular settlement. What makes mediation exciting, from a cultural standpoint, is its impartiality and neutrality. In addition, the mediator does not expect to benefit directly from either party. The actual mediation activity proceeds through twelve stages, beginning with an initial contracting between the parties and ending with an evaluation of the formal settlement. This formal process permits all persons to reach an agreement in a friendly (and, hopefully, painless) manner. Organizational or personal conflicts may be resolved expeditiously through mediation.

Student affairs professionals must involve minority students in meaningful campus activities, both minority-only and cross-race activities. Too often, minority student activities are limited to participation in minority-oriented organizations. While these student organizations play a vital role by giving minorities a sense of camaraderie and belonging, especially on predominantly white campuses, they can limit minority-white interactions to superficial relationships.

Student activities programming should foster cultural pluralism and illustrate the significance of having minorities on campus. For example, at Pennsylvania State University, white and minority students volunteer to become members of the Student Government Race Relations Board.

These students are trained to present racial and gender awareness programs to residence halls, fraternities, sororities, classes, and community groups. Pennsylvania State University also has established the Martin Luther King, Jr., residential interest house. House members focus on moral development and nonviolent means of social change. This interest house provides a viable alternative for many students. The campus offers a human relations activity, the Ebony and Ivory Program, which provides students with opportunities to discuss ways of improving their ability to communicate with culturally different people.

Residence life staff may be in a unique position to sculpt living environments and sponsor activities that celebrate minority group diversity. Activities that facilitate minority intergroup interactions or explore values or beliefs promote a healthy living environment for all students. During new-student orientation periods at Pennsylvania State University, students are offered a wide range of programs, all designed to increase their level of human relations awareness. For many, the university environment provides the first opportunity to have meaningful interactions with a culturally diverse population. Also, these students need to be taught the interpersonal skills to manage these interactions successfully. Currently, residence life programs at Pennsylvania State University require each residence assistant to offer at least one human relations program during the fall. This activity seems to set a positive tone for the inclusion of minority students in all house activities.

Training. The importance of human relations training for faculties and professional and clerical staff has increased over the past few years as a result of students' requests for cultural sensitivity in classrooms and in support activities. Training programs should not only focus on cultural similarities but also should applaud persons who have diverse cross-cultural skills. Human relations training programs encourage participants to explore their own life experiences and understand how those experiences have affected their abilities to respond to racism and cultural differences.

Such student training should avoid focusing only on the "victim" of prejudice and should emphasize instead how students may survive racial prejudice. This training effort could be altered to fit participants' levels of awareness and their personal program goals. Pennsylvania State University currently offers a range of human relations training workshops that have been effective with students, resident assistants, staff, and faculty. The advantage of these workshops is that they do not require experts in human relations theory and practice. On the contrary, training programs presented by facilitators, who present themselves as individuals concerned about and wrestling with their own prejudices, are most effective.

Other Student Affairs Activities. Student affairs programs and services extend beyond counseling, and cross-cultural counseling skills may be transferred easily to other student affairs units. Financial aid advisers, for example, may serve their clienteles better if they recognize and understand minority students' financial and social needs. College union professionals, given a basic knowledge of their own values, the institution's values, and those of minority students, may offer events and support campus organizations that serve the needs of all students effectively and fairly. Pedersen noted ten frequent manifestations of cultural bias: assumptions regarding normal behaviors; emphasis on individualism; fragmentation of academic disciplines; all Western cultures' dependence on abstract concepts; overemphasis on independence; neglect of clients' support systems; dependence on linear thinking; focus on changing the individual, not systems; neglect of history; and the danger of cultural encapsulation (Pedersen, 1987). Training programs that focus on changing these ten factors enhance the ability of student affairs professionals to work effectively with all students. Through the basic techniques of cross-cultural counseling (questioning, becoming aware of one's values, recognizing and respecting the values of minorities, and adjusting one's behavior to minority students), student affairs professionals can expand their skills to work effectively with minorities, regardless of specific services provided.

Working with Faculty. Student affairs units do not exist in a vacuum. Problems that minority students experience in the classroom often extend to their personal and social lives. For this reason, student affairs professionals should familiarize themselves with faculty-minority interactions. The results of a workshop (Association of American Colleges, 1984) identified several areas of classroom frustration for black students: feelings of alienation and lack of acceptance; lack of positive references to blacks or black culture and black contributions; lack of black role models in faculty and administrative positions; subtle as well as overt challenges to the competence of black students, and racial assumptions that some white faculty bring to the classroom; and difficulty in being accepted as an individual by many white students who, like some faculty, harbor certain assumptions about blacks. Often faculty members have unrealistic or faulty expectations of minority students; some faculty believe minorities will make few classroom contributions, while others expect minority students to learn classroom material with no special assistance.

Often minority students enter college with academic deficiencies that they do not know how to overcome. Many enter with the expectation—frequently a misconception—that the institution will respond to their academic needs. Some minority students are naive about the university's responsibility to them and they bring this naiveté into student affairs offices, as well as bringing issues more legitimately viewed as student affairs concerns. By increasing our interactions with academic departments and by verbalizing our concerns, we can increase our institutions' capacity to serve minority students.

Minority student retention is or should be of concern to the entire institution. Minority students' adjustment to the campus environment is contingent on their academic success in some cases. Minority students often have three common expectations of white faculty members. They expect faculty members to interact with them in a nonracist manner, help white students understand that negative attitudes toward minority students are wrong, and present information regarding the contributions of ethnic minority groups. A faculty awareness workshop developed at Pennsylvania State University helps faculty increase their racial sensitivity. This workshop stresses improving faculty's ability to relate with new awareness to minority students. For developing a similar workshop, some guidelines are useful:

1. Do not mix faculty, staff, and students together in a workshop. Faculty members seem to view their concerns as special and are likely to benefit more from a faculty-only workshop.
2. Workshops that have the support and participation of the institution's leadership are most successful.
3. Faculty persons are generally the most effective workshop leaders.
4. The workshop design should model appropriate faculty behaviors in meeting with minority students.
5. The presentation of information alone, without practice, will not change faculty behaviors toward minority students.

Conclusion

Minority students of tomorrow will continue to change professionals' perceptions of the traditional college student. In the next decade, the institutions that are best able to alter their programs and services and to accommodate minority students will enjoy stable student enrollment and high-quality student affairs programs.

Focusing on minority students' academic, social, and developmental needs is not an issue of social consciousness only, but also one of institutional survival. Building for the future, using methods from the past, leaves institutions behind when they need to be in the forefront. Toffler (1970) noted that the "half-life" of a graduate engineer was approximately ten years; that is, within a decade, half of his or her knowledge would be outdated. Today that half-life is even shorter. Human services fields, including student affairs, may have a similar timetable. If this perception is accurate, then programs that prepare graduate students to work with a static college population miseducate their students. More important, they fail to prepare them to promote development for white and minority-students.

Over the years, minority-white peer relations have been fraught with misunderstanding and confusion, but that history is ending. As white students become more informed about the cultural backgrounds, histories,

and language differences of our country's minority groups, they may begin
to appreciate and demand cultural diversity in their campus learning and
living environments.

When minority students achieve acceptance on college campuses,
they will renew trust in their interactions with white peers. By doing so,
minority students will enjoy an increased sense of belonging to previously
all-white campuses. Minority and white students and the entire campus
will profit.

The by-product of enhanced minority-white relations on campus is
an enlightened, dynamic learning environment rich in cultural diversity.
Minority students add to higher education a vitality essential to colleges'
survival. Enhancing minority-white peer interactions is a vision for higher
education; for its minority students, it is an achievable goal in the years to
come.

References

Association of American Colleges. *White Faculty-Black Students: Exploring Assumptions and Practice.* Washington, D.C.: Association of American Colleges, 1984.

Banks, J. A. *Education in the 80s: Multiethnic Education.* Washington, D.C.: National Education Association, 1981.

Beckman, B. *The Black Student's Guide to College.* Providence, R.I.: Beckman-Harris, 1984.

Council for the Advancement of Standards for Student Services/Student Development Programs. *CAS Standards and Guidelines for Student Services/Student Development Programs.* Washington, D.C.: Consortium of Student Affairs Professional Organizations, 1986.

Fleming, J. *Blacks in College: A Comparative Study of Students' Success in Black and in White Institutions.* San Francisco: Jossey-Bass, 1984.

Gibbs, J. T. "Black Students at Integrated Colleges: Problems and Prospects." In C. V. Willie (ed.), *Black, Brown, White Relations: Race Relations in the 1970s.* New Brunswick, N.J.: Transaction Books, 1977.

Griscom, J. L. "Sex, Race, and Class: Three Dimensions of a Woman's Experience." *Counseling Psychologist,* 1979, *8* (1), 10-11.

Hocker, J. L., and Wilmot, W. W. *Interpersonal Conflict.* Dubuque, Iowa: Brown, 1985.

June, L. N., and Pringle, G. D. "The Concept of Race in the Career Development Theories of Roe, Super, and Holland." *Journal of Non-White Concerns in Personnel and Guidance,* 1977, *6* (1), 17-23.

Katz, J. *White Awareness: Handbook for Anti-Racism Training.* Norman: University of Oklahoma Press, 1978.

Margolis, R. L., and Rungta, S. A. "Training Counselors for Work with Special Populations: A Second Look." *Journal of Counseling and Development,* 1986, *64* (10), 642-644.

Moore, C. W. *The Mediation Process: Practical Strategies for Resolving Conflict.* San Francisco: Jossey-Bass, 1986.

Pedersen, P. "Trial Counseling." In R. Corsini (ed.), *Handbook of Innovative Psychotherapies.* New York: Wiley-Interscience, 1981.

Pedersen, P. "Counseling Clients from Other Cultures: Two Training Designs." In

M. K. Asante, E. Newmark, and C. A. Black (eds.), *Handbook of Intercultural Communication.* Beverly Hills, Calif.: Sage, 1987.

Peterson, M. W., Blackburn, B., Garrison, R., Arce, J., Davenport, T., and Mingle, M. *Black Students on White Campuses: The Impact of Increased Black Enrollments.* Ann Arbor, Mich.: Institute for Social Research, 1978.

Ting-Toomey, S., "Toward a Theory of Conflict and Culture." In W. B. Gudykunst, L. P. Steward, and S. Ting-Toomey (eds.), *Communication, Culture, and Organizational Process.* Beverly Hills, Calif.: Sage, 1985.

Toffler, A. *Future Shock.* New York: Random House, 1970.

Turner, R. D. "The Resurgence of Racism on White Campuses." *The Black Collegian,* 1985, *4* (2), 18-24.

Wilzosh, L. "Beyond Counseling Women: Some Contemporary Issues." *International Journal for the Advancement of Counseling,* 1983, *6,* 125-133.

W. Terrell Jones is assistant director of the Division of Campus Life and affiliate assistant professor in the Counselor Education Department at the Pennsylvania State University.

Several key recommendations are offered, as well as annotated references for enhancing programs and services to minority students.

Summary and Annotated References

Doris J. Wright

Undeniably, the increase in minority college enrollment is directly attributable to the early civil rights movement's efforts to achieve basic college education entitlements and to ensure access to affordable college education. Success in this area led to the creation of "special" services and programs aimed at instilling pride in ethnic heritage. While this success was a historical breakthrough, these strategies are no longer sufficient to support tomorrow's diverse group of minority students, who are now preparing to accept their leadership roles in the twentieth-first century. As the authors featured in this volume have pointed out, student affairs practitioners now fill the enviable role of forerunners in this dramatic change. They face a dual challenge: to question the efficacy of their current approaches to minority education and academic excellence, and to shift their thinking accordingly. The following are recommendations for student affairs practitioners and concerned others.

Recommendations

1. Student affairs practitioners can no longer assume minority group homogeneity. American ethnic minority groups are diverse and heterogeneous in customs, values, linguistic styles, and social or economic

D. J. Wright (ed.). *Responding to the Needs of Today's Minority Students.*
New Directions for Student Services, no. 38. San Francisco: Jossey-Bass, Summer 1987.

class. Therefore, minority programs and services should reflect this heterogeneity in their activities.

2. With increasingly diverse ethnicity on campus, colleges can no longer assume that the traditional student entering college from high school will be white, especially if those colleges are located in the Southwest, the West, and major urban centers in the Northeast. Consequently, student affairs practitioners must ensure that all written, oral, and visual communication media reflect this demographic shift.

3. Assumption of a more ethnically diverse campus requires the re-education of student affairs practitioners, staff, and faculty with regard to this cultural and ethnic diversity and its impact on service delivery and classroom instruction. Further, colleges should hold campuswide cross-cultural training activities for all staff and faculty and should evaluate cross-cultural competencies as part of hiring, promotion, and merit decisions.

4. Student affairs practitioners should be made aware of institutional policy changes brought about by legal and ethical issues or by legislation, particularly affirmative action laws. Moreover, practitioners should be advised of changes in ethical standards that address respect for and familiarity with minority groups—for example, the CAS standards and guidelines, which set forth policies for provision of services to and interaction with minority groups (see appendixes 1 and 2).

5. Student affairs staff should conduct institutional research into the effectiveness of minority student developmental tasks involving "minority only" activities, as well as those facilitated by participation in "mainstream" programs or services (which include both minority and nonminority students). During financial crises, such research could strengthen arguments for the maintenance of minority-oriented programs, as well as providing information about the learning and developmental patterns of minority students.

6. Research has suggested that continued development of support resources (such as ethnic studies and cultural awareness programs) that enhance minority students' cultural identity is a critical variable in the retention and graduation of ethnic minorities. Student affairs units must develop creative ways to maintain and expand such support resources, especially during times of fiscal retrenchment. Such resources should be included in permanent university budgets, thereby removing these programs from "soft" funding.

7. Studies of minority students have shown that an important ingredient in their college survival is the involvement of minority staff and faculty with minority students. Minority faculty contribute to the student's sense of belonging and provide adult role models that may be emulated later. This finding suggests a need for more intensive minority recruitment, directed toward visibility of minority faculty and staff in all areas, including the upper posts in student affairs administration.

8. Colleges and universities have overlooked an important resource in the recruitment and graduation of minority students: parents and families. In student affairs activities involving minorities, the inclusion of parents and other family members could provide practitioners with a valuable resource for understanding minority students' unique learning, social, and cultural needs. Moreover, minority parents, if assured that the institution will support their children, can become some of the institution's most enthusiastic supporters and recruiters. Student affairs units should seek creative ways to involve parents in their children's education. For example, they might invite parents to attend weekend events (athletic or otherwise) where they could meet student affairs staff and have small-group discussion on topics of mutual interest. The dialogue, to be entirely successful, must be a two-way interaction, with parents and student affairs staff alike receiving the benefits.

9. The recently published CAS standards and guidelines for student affairs programs (see appendixes 1 and 2) provide direction for the implementation of services to minority students. Institutions of all types and sizes must be encouraged to comply with the CAS standards and to ensure that their professionals are competent enough to work with minorities. Also, student affairs programs should seek consultation whenever they are uncertain about the quality of their programs for minority students. A peer review process to monitor minority services might provide student affairs administrators feedback concerning their programs.

Conclusions

As predominantly white institutions approach the twenty-first century, their continued growth depends on their success in attracting and graduating minority students, who represent the "traditional" college student of the future. The thriving colleges and universities of the next century will be those that have responded to the developmental, academic, and social needs of minority students. In these minority students rests our country's future leadership. By providing high-quality programs and services to mold these minority students into skilled, competent, caring leaders, student affairs professionals can maintain their present reputation as innovative leaders in higher education.

Annotated References

Allen, W. R. "Black Student, White Campus: Structural, Interpersonal, and Psychological Correlates of Success." *Journal of Negro Education*, 1985, *54* (2), 139–147.

This study examines structural, interpersonal, and psychological correlates of student outcomes in a national sample of black undergraduates drawn from six predominantly white, state-supported universities. Strategies for black students' successful adaptation to college life are recommended.

Asante, M. K., Newmark, E., and Blake, C. A. (eds.). *Handbook of Intercultural Communications.* Beverly Hills, Calif.: Sage, 1977.

This interdisciplinary reference book presents many different views of intercultural communication and makes suggestions for practical application. The author builds a foundation on which knowledge of human interactions can be accumulated. The book covers theoretical considerations, conceptual frameworks, issues in intercultural communication, general problems and data, research in specific cultures, and practical application and training methods.

Brislen, R. W., Cushner, K., Cherrie, C., and Young, M. *Intercultural Interactions: A Practical Guide.* Beverly Hills, Calif.: Sage, 1986.

The most "applied" volume in a series on cross-cultural research and methodology, this book is an excellent training resource to assist individuals in making the transition from one culture to another.

Brown, A. D. "Adjustment Programs for the American Indian College Student." In *Contemporary American Indian Issues in Higher Education.* Los Angeles: University of California, American Indian Studies Center, 1981.

This article examines the problems that American Indian students experience in adjusting to college. Support programs that strive to meet the needs of Indian students are briefly discussed. The author offers a number of recommendations to improve college programs for Indian students.

Chu, J., and Sue, S. "Asian/Pacific Americans and Group Practice." *Social Work with Groups,* 1984, 7 (3), 23–26.

This outstanding article addresses cultural factors and historical background as significant concerns in working with Asian Americans. Considerable attention is devoted to the importance of understanding and appreciating group strategies, values, and dynamics.

Council for the Advancement of Standards for Student Services/Student Development Programs. *CAS Standards and Guidelines for Student Services/Student Development Programs.* Washington, D.C.: Consortium of Student Affairs Professional Organizations, April 1986.

This document articulates the minimum standards for establishing and maintaining student affairs programs in all collegiate settings and recommends guidelines for how standards should be enforced. This reference is an absolute "must" for practitioners, administrators, and graduate students in student affairs.

Cox, T., Jr. "Blacks and Higher Education: Where Do We Stand and What Difference Does It Make Anyway?" *The Negro Educational Review*, 1983, *33* (3), 146–160.

This article examines and discusses data on higher education of black Americans that may be helpful in assessing not only the actual progress of blacks relative to whites in higher education but also the all-important issue of the value of college in improving the quality of life for black Americans.

Cummings, T. "The Report of Engineering Special Programs, July 1, 1983–June 30, 1984." (ED 251 255)

The author describes the University of New Mexico's efforts to achieve ethnic parity for underrepresented minorities in its College of Engineering. Recruitment and retention efforts in precollege programs, in the Math, Engineering, and Science Achievement (MESA) program, and in undergraduate programs are outlined.

Deal, T. E., and Kennedy, A. A. *Corporate Cultures: The Rites and Rituals of Corporate Life*. Reading, Mass.: Addison-Wesley, 1982.

Deal and Kennedy have provided an excellent tool for the evaluation of an institution's culture. In general, their model holds to the theory that all organizations can be viewed as cultures. Each culture has implicit and explicit values, heroes, rites and rituals, and communication networks. This book suggests that institutions of higher education, as cultures, can be changed through a process of self-diagnosis. By identifying existing institutional concepts that support change, one can begin to reshape the present culture. This process allows practitioners to devise change strategies that are culture-specific.

Falk, D. R., and Aitken, L. P. "Promoting Retention Among American Indian College Students." *Journal of American Indian Education*, 1984, *23* (2), 24–31.

The authors interviewed 125 Chippewa Indian students and 11 educators from institutions with large Chippewa student enrollment to identify factors promoting retention of American Indian college students. Five factors are identified and briefly discussed, including developmental academic-preparation programs; institutional commitment, beginning with top-level administrators; and more complete financial aid packages.

Gee, E. *Counterpoint: Perspectives on Asian Americans*. Los Angeles: Asian American Studies Center, Resource Development and Publications, University of California, 1976.

In this exciting anthology, the Asian American experience is depicted in sections: critical perspectives, contemporary issues, and literature reviews.

This is an excellent text focusing on topical issues, education, communications and mass media, land, labor and capital, and recent immigration.

Jones, P. E. (ed.). *Historical Perspectives on the Development of Equal Opportunity in Higher Education.* Iowa City, Iowa: The American College Testing Program, 1978.

This book provides discussion to stimulate the thinking of faculty, counselors, and administrators and encourage them to develop greater awareness of issues affecting equal opportunity in higher education. The editorial style of this publication reflects the informal atmosphere of its sponsoring organization.

Katz, J. *White Awareness: Handbook for Anti-Racism Training.* Norman: University of Oklahoma Press, 1978.

Although somewhat dated, this remains one of the best step-by-step models on anti-racism training. This work was designed for educators, counselors, and facilitators who are concerned about social change. It focuses on racism as a "white" problem and suggests ways of changing it. The book provides the practitioner with a six-stage program of designed activities that will move a group from awareness to positive action.

LaFromboise, T. D., and Dixon, D. N. "American Indian Perception of Trustworthiness in a Counseling Interview." *Journal of Counseling Psychology,* 1981, *28* (2), 135–139.

This study involved forty-four American Indian high school students who viewed videotapes of in-session counseling behavior and rated counselors on perceived trustworthiness. The effect of a counselor's race on students' perceived trustworthiness is also examined. The findings indicate that behaviors associated with perceived trustworthiness can be adopted. Thus, counselors can be trained to exhibit specific behaviors that will indicate trustworthiness.

Lee, P., Juan, G., and Hom, A. "Group Work Practice with Asians: A Sociocultural Approach." *Social Work with Groups,* 1984, *7* (3), 37–48.

This investigative article utilizes a sociocultural approach to working with Asian Americans, suggesting the importance of a working knowledge of Asian American heritage, a respect for family members in the group process, and an awareness of the significance of role expectation in group dynamics. This is an excellent description of culture and a practical approach for group processes with Asian Americans.

Leong, F. "Career Development of Asian Americans." *Journal of College Student Personnel,* 1985, *26*, 539–546.

This article critically reviews the empirical and theoretical literature on the career development of Asian Americans. It clearly defines the issues of conflict for Asian American students.

Leong, F. "Counseling and Psychotherapy with Asian Americans: Review of the Literature." *Journal of Counseling Psychology*, 1986, *33* (2), 196–206.

This is an excellent discussion of issues concerning Asian Americans. The references listed in this article are extensive and represent the major work done in this area.

Maynard, M. "Can Universities Adapt to Ethnic Minority Students' Needs?" *Journal of College Student Personnel*, 1980, *21* (4), 398–401.

This article addresses some issues concerning the adaptability of universities in meeting the needs of ethnic minority students and suggests program strategies that are beneficial both for students and for the university milieu.

Pedersen, P. (ed.). *Handbook of Cross-Cultural Counseling and Therapy.* Westport, Conn.: Greenwood Press, 1985.

This is an excellent reference book, with concise contributions from some of the most prominent authors on cross-cultural counseling and therapy. The forty contributions are subdivided into five areas of emphasis: the conceptual focus of cross-cultural counseling, alternative counseling methods, client populations, culture-sensitive issues, and education and training issues.

Pedersen, P. "Ten Frequent Assumptions of Cultural Bias in Counseling." *Journal of Multicultural Counseling and Development*, 1987, *1*, 16–24.

This article discusses assumptions about counselors' cultural biases and makes recommendations for managing bias.

Ploski, H. A., and Kaiser, E. (eds.). *Afro USA: A Reference Work on the Black Experience.* New York: Bellwether, 1971.

This book seeks to provide the widest possible audience with an accurate, comprehensive, and well-documented study of black culture in the United States and around the world.

Visual Communications of Asian American Studies Central, Inc., 244 South San Pedro, Los Angeles, California.

This Asian American company specializes in films and videos about the Asian American experience. California is used as the setting in many cases. The products are thought-provoking and often heartwarming.

Wright, B. "Programming Success: Special Student Services and the American Indian College Student." *Journal of American Indian Education,* 1985, *24* (1), 1-7.

Programmatic efforts to advance equity in higher education for disadvantaged students, particularly American Indian students, are examined. Academic support services, counseling support services, ethnic studies, student centers and organizations, and faculty and administrator roles are discussed. Ways to strengthen existing efforts are also described.

Doris J. Wright is a staff psychologist at the Counseling and Mental Health Center at the University of Texas at Austin. Since 1970, she has worked with minority students on six campuses. She writes frequently on minority student developments.

APPENDIX 1
CAS Standards and Guidelines for
Student Services/Development Programs:
General Standards

General Standards

The Council for the Advancement of Standards for Student Services/Development Programs (CAS) developed and adopted standards and interpretive guidelines for specific functional areas of student services/development programs within post-secondary educational institutions.

There are important General Standards that govern the activities of all student services/development programs. These General Standards are integral to each functional area. **Thus, each functional area standards and guidelines must be interpreted and applied in conjunction with the General Standards below.**

Since institutions vary in size, character, location, and type of students, the organization and nature of student services/development programs will vary. Accordingly, each specific standard and its related guidelines must be read and interpreted in the context of the unique characteristics of the institution. Nonetheless, all standards are intended to apply regardless of organizational differences.

General Standards for Student Services/Development Programs

Mission

Each institution and each functional area must develop, review, and disseminate regularly its own specific goals for student services/development, which must be consistent with the nature and goals of the institution and with the standards in this document.

Program

The overall student services/development program must be (a) purposeful, (b) coherent, (c) based upon or related to theories and knowledge of human development and learning characteristics, and (d) reflective of the demographic and developmental profiles of the student body. Such programs and services must (a) promote student development by encouraging such things as positive and realistic self-appraisal, intellectual development, appropriate personal and occupational choices, clarification of values, physical fitness, the ability to relate meaningfully with others, the capacity to engage in a personally satisfying and effective style of living, the capacity to appreciate cultural and aesthetic differences, and the capacity to work independently and interdependently; (b) assist students in overcoming specific personal, physical, or educational problems or skill deficiencies; and (c) identify environmental conditions that may negatively influence welfare and propose interventions that may neutralize such conditions. The educational experience of students consists of both academic efforts in the classroom and developmental opportunities through student services and development programs. Institutions must define the relative importance of these processes.

Leadership and Management

The institution must appoint a chief student services/development officer or designate an individual to fulfill that role. This leader must be positioned in the organization so that the needs of the students and the functional areas are well represented at the highest administrative level of the institution. This leader must be an experienced and effective manager, must have substantial work experience in one or more of the student services/development functional areas, and either be an acknowledged leader on the campus or have obvious background and experience to command such respect. The specific title and reporting relationship of this individual may vary among institutions. The individual must be selected on the basis of personal characteristics and formal training.

The officer must create an effective system to manage the services/programs. The officer must plan, organize, staff, lead, and assess programs on a continuing basis. The result should be an integrated system of student services and development activities for the institution, funded and otherwise supported at a level that permits the effective delivery of these programs.

The officer must be able to develop, to advocate, and to use a statement of mission, goals, and objectives for student services/development on the campus. The officer must attract and select qualified staff members who make effective decisions about policies, procedures, personnel, budgets, facilities, and equipment. The officer must assume responsibilities for program and personnel development, assessment, and improvement of the services and development activities of the organization.

Organization and Administration

Each functional area must have its own set of policies and procedures that include a detailed description of the administrative process of the office and an organizational chart showing the job functions and reporting relationships within and beyond the functional area.

Human Resources

Each functional area must have adequate and qualified professional staff to fulfill the mission of that service and to implement all aspects of the program. To be qualified, professional staff members must have a graduate degree in a field of study relevant to the particular job in question or must have an appropriate combination of education and experience. In any functional area in which there is a full-time director, that director must possess levels of education and/or professional experience beyond that of the staff to be supervised.

Preprofessional or support staff members employed in a functional area must be qualified by relevant education and experience. Degree requirements, including both degree levels and subject matter, must be germane to the particular job responsibilities. Such staff members must be trained appropriately and supervised adequately by professional staff.

Paraprofessionals must be carefully selected, trained with respect to helping skills and institutional services and procedures, closely supervised, and evaluated regularly. Their compensation must be fair and any voluntary services must be recognized adequately. Paraprofessionals must recognize the limitations of their knowledge and skills and must refer students to appropriate professionals when the problems encountered warrant.

To ensure that professional staff members devote adequate time to professional duties, each functional area must have sufficient clerical and technical support staff. Such support must be of sufficient quantity and quality to accomplish the following kinds of activities: typing, filing, telephone and other receptionist duties, bookkeeping, maintaining student records, organizing resource materials, receiving students and making appointments, and handling routine correspondence.

Salary level and fringe benefits for staff must be commensurate with those for similar professional, preprofessional, and clerical positions at the institution and in the geographic area.

To ensure the existence of suitable and readily identifiable role models within the campus teaching and administrative ranks, staff employment profiles must reflect representation of categories of persons who comprise the student population. However, where student bodies are predominantly nondisabled, of one race, sex, or religion, a diverse staffing pattern will enrich the teaching/administrative ranks and will demonstrate institutional commitment to fair employment practices.

All functional areas must have a regular system of staff selection and evaluation, and must provide continuing professional development opportunities for staff including in-service training programs, participation in professional conferences, workshops, and other continuing education activities.

Funding

Each functional area must have funding sufficient to carry out its mission and to support the following, where applicable: staff salaries; purchase and maintenance of office furnishings, supplies, materials, and equipment, including current technology; phone and postage costs; printing and media costs; institutional memberships in appropriate professional organizations; relevant subscriptions and necessary library resources; attendance at professional association meetings, conferences, and workshops; and other professional development activities. In addition to institutional funding commitment through general funds, other funding sources may be considered, including: state appropriations, student fees, user fees, donations and contributions, fines, concession and store sales, rentals, and dues.

Facilities

Each functional area must be provided adequate facilities to fulfill its mission. As applicable, the facilities for each functional area must include, or the function must have access to, the following: private offices or private spaces for counseling, interviewing, or other meetings of a confidential nature; office, reception and storage space sufficient to accommodate assigned staff, supplies, equipment, library resources, and machinery; and conference room or meeting space. All facilities must be accessible to disabled persons and must be in compliance with relevant federal, state, and local health and safety requirements.

Legal Responsibilities

Staff members must be knowledgeable about and responsive to relevant civil and criminal laws and must be responsible for ensuring that the institution fulfills its legal obligations. Staff members in all functional areas must be well versed in those obligations and limitations imposed on the operation of the institution, particularly in their functional area, by federal, state, and local constitutional, statutory, regulatory, and common law, and by institutional policy. They must utilize appropriate policies and practices to limit the liability exposure of the institution, its officers, employees, and agents. The institution must provide access to legal advice to professional staff as needed to carry out assigned responsibilities.

Equal Opportunity, Access, and Affirmative Action

Each functional area must adhere to the spirit and intent of equal opportunity laws in all activities. Each area must ensure that its services and facilities are accessible to and provide hours of operation that respond to the needs of special student populations, including cultural and special needs subgroups, evening, part-time, and commuter students.

Personnel policies shall not discriminate on the basis of race, sex, color, religion, age, national origin, and/or handicap. In hiring and promotion policies, student services professionals must take affirmative action that strives to remedy significant staffing imbalances, particularly when resulting from past discriminatory practices. Each functional area must seek to identify, prevent, and/or remedy other discriminatory practices.

Campus and Community Relations

Each functional area must maintain good relations with relevant campus offices and external agencies, which necessarily requires regular identification of the offices with which such relationships are critical.

Multicultural Programs and Services

The institution must provide to members of its majority and minority cultures educational efforts that focus on awareness of cultural differences, self-assessment of possible prejudices, and desirable behavioral changes. The institution also must provide educational programs for minority students that identify their unique needs, prioritize those needs, and respond to the priorities to the degree that numbers of students, facilities, and resources permit. In addition, the institution must orient minority students to the culture of the institution and promote and deepen their understanding of their own culture and heritage.

Ethics

All persons involved in the provision of services to students must maintain the highest standards of ethical behavior. Staff members of each functional area must develop or adopt standards of ethical practice addressing the unique problems that face personnel in that area. The standards must be published and reviewed by all concerned. In the formulation of those standards, ethical standards statements previously adopted by the profession at large or relevant professional associations may be of assistance and must be considered.

Certain ethical obligations apply to all individuals employed in student services/development programs, for example:

> All staff members must ensure that confidentiality is maintained with respect to all communications and records considered confidential. Unless written permission is given by the student, information disclosed in individual counseling sessions must remain confidential. In addition, all requirements of the *Family Educational Rights and Privacy Act* (Buckley Amendment) must be complied with and information contained in students' educational records must not be disclosed to third parties without appropriate consent, unless one of the relevant statutory exceptions applies. A similar dedication to privacy and confidentiality must be applied to research data concerning individuals.

> All staff members must be aware of and comply with the provisions contained in the institution's human subjects policy and in any other institutional policy addressing ethical practices.

All staff members must ensure that students are provided access to services on a fair and equitable basis.

All staff members must avoid any personal conflict of interest so they can deal objectively and impartially with persons within and outside the institution. In many instances, the appearance of a conflict of interest can be as damaging as an actual conflict.

Whenever handling funds, all staff members must ensure that such funds are handled in accordance with established and responsible accounting procedures.

Staff members must not participate in any form of sexual harassment. Sexual harassment is defined to include sexual advances, requests for sexual favors, as well as other verbal or physical conduct of a sexual nature if (1) submission to such conduct is made either explicitly or implicitly a term or condition of an individual's employment, academic progress, or any other outcome of an official nature, (2) . . . is used as the basis for such decisions or outcomes . . . , (3) . . . has

the purpose or effect of unreasonably interfering with an individual's work performance or creating an intimidating, hostile, or offensive working environment. (29 Code of Federal Regulations, C.F.R., Section 1604.11 (a).)

All staff members must recognize the limits of their training, expertise, and competence and must refer students in need of further expertise to persons possessing appropriate qualifications.

Evaluation

There must be systematic and regular research and evaluation of the overall institutional student services/development program and each functional area to determine whether the educational goals and the needs of students are being met. Although methods of evaluation may vary, they must utilize both quantitative and qualitative measures. Data collected must include responses from students and other significant constituencies. Results of these regular evaluations must be used in revising and improving the program goals and implementation.

Those using this document for the purposes of self-study or other program development are advised that the **General Standards** are those elements found in common to the several functional area standards and guidelines. While of potential utility as a stand-alone document, the **General Standards** are not so designed. These **General Standards** must be read with the functional area standards and guidelines addressing the following: **Academic Advising, Career Planning and Placement, College Unions, Commuter Student Programs and Services, Counseling Services, Disabled Student Services, Fraternity and Sorority Advising, Housing and Residential Life Programs, Judicial Programs and Services, Learning Assistance Programs, Minority Student Programs and Services, Recreational Sports, Religious Programs, Research and Evaluation, Student Activities, and Student Orientation Programs.**

Prepared by the Council for the Advancement of Standards for Student Services/Development Programs, 1986.

APPENDIX 2
CAS Standards and Guidelines for Student Services/Development Programs: Minority Student Programs and Services

Mission

See General Standards

The provision of minority student programs and services should presuppose a strong campus sense of a *common* community, serving all its citizens fairly, and marked in the main by:

—access to, rather than exclusion from, academic, social, and recreational groups and activities;

—shared goals;

—intentional social intercourse, rather than passive social isolation or active social exclusion; and

—integration rather than segregation.

On those campuses with minority student programs and services, the program must promote the academic and personal growth and development of the various minority students served.

To accomplish the mission, the goals of the program must be to:

■ assess the needs of minority students in selected areas, set priorities among those needs, and respond to the extent that the number of students, facilities, and resources permit;

■ orient minority students to the culture of the institution;

■ assist minority students to determine and assess their educational goals and academic skills;

■ provide support services to help minority students achieve educational goals and attain or refine academic skills necessary to perform adequately in the classroom;

■ promote the intellectual, career, social, and moral development of the students;

■ promote and deepen each minority student's understanding of his or her own culture and heritage;

■ promote and deepen majority students' understanding of minority students' cultures and heritages;

■ provide training in leadership skills and other personal and social skills for minority students and those seeking to assist them; and

■ offer or identify appropriate minority mentors and role models.

In addition, the program must provide educational efforts for both majority and minority students that focus on:

■ awareness of cultural differences;

■ self-assessment of cultural awareness and possible prejudices; and

■ changing prejudicial attitudes or behaviors.

The program can include efforts supplementary to other institutional functional areas such as recruitment, placement, academic advising, counseling, and alumni relations.

Staff members in minority programs and services should coordinate their efforts with academic units and other student affairs areas.

It is important not to look upon minority student programs and services as the only organized agency to meet the needs of minority students. All institutional units should be responsible for meeting the needs of minority students in their areas of responsibility.

Coordinated efforts to promote multicultural sensitivity and the elimination of prejudicial behaviors should be made at every institution by all functional areas.

Program

See General Standards

Minority student programs and services must include the following elements:

■ **Assessment of the educational goals, academic skills, personal developmental levels, and social, recreational, and cultural needs of minority students**

Assessments may be carried out in many ways. Survey instruments, interviews, behavioral tests, observations, or some combination of these methods may be appropriate in a given institution.

■ **Educational programs to enhance the knowledge, understanding, and skills necessary for academic success**

Educational programming should both complement the academic interests of the students, and be based upon assessments of the students and demands of the institution's educational programs. It may be provided in collaboration with efforts by academic departments or schools and other service offices.

■ **Educational programs to enhance the knowledge, understanding, and skills necessary for personal development**

Activities which attempt to promote the career, social, recreational, and moral development of students should be based upon assessments and should also reflect unique dimensions of the minority student experience.

Social and recreational programs should enhance the knowledge, understanding, and skills necessary for social success, the productive use of leisure time, and the development of satisfying interpersonal relationships.

Recreational programs should be designed to promote physical health, leisure time enjoyment, and psychological well-being of students.

For both social skills and recreational programs, proper emphasis should be placed on any unique needs or cultural expressions of social relationships and recreational activities.

■ **Educational programs to enhance the knowledge, understanding, and skills necessary for the exercise of leadership**

Leadership programs should be designed to help individuals understand the components and styles of leadership.

■ **Supplemental orientation programming to enhance knowledge and understanding of the purposes of the institution, its values, and predictable ways of behaving**

This program should help students assess the degree of congruence between their educational goals and skills and the culture of the institution. It also should emphasize programs and services available in the institution to help students achieve the knowledge, understanding, and skills necessary to perform adequately, both in and out of the classroom.

- **Programming to enhance the knowledge and understanding of each student's own culture and heritage**

  These programs should explore both the heritage and current expressions of the student's culture.

  Various dimensions of the student's culture, such as history, philosophy, world view, literature, and various forms of artistic expression, should be explored.

- **Human relations programming to explore awareness of cultural differences, self-assessment of possible prejudices, and the facilitation of desired behavioral changes**

  Human relations programs should be designed to assist both majority and minority students, faculty, and staff to develop more tolerance, understanding, and ability to relate to others.

- **Advocacy within the institution for minority student life experiences and organizations**

  Tacit or overt prejudices or discriminations against minority students should be challenged.

  Sometimes institutions espouse one point of view but practice knowingly or unknowingly another. If the practical effects of policies are prejudicial, then staff members should bring these facts to the attention of the proper authorities in the institution.

  Impediments to the growth and development of minority students or full participation of minorities within the institution should be identified and addressed.

- **Advising of groups and individual students**

  Advising services may include, but are not limited to:

  —monitoring scholastic standing of groups and individual students and recommending programs for improvement;

  —providing workshops, programs, retreats, and seminars on relevant topics and encouraging attendance at activities and services sponsored by other campus offices;

  —encouraging attendance at conferences, meetings, and programs;

  —advising formal groups such as editorial staffs of minority newspapers or newsletters, fraternal groups, preprofessional clubs, and program councils;

  —providing assistance and advice in planning of minority student celebrations (e.g., Hispanic Week or Black History Month);

  —assisting minority student groups or individuals in identifying and gaining access, where appropriate, to institutional services such as printing, bulk mailing, and computer services;

  —providing a directory of minority faculty and staff; and

  —publishing a newsletter which focuses on current events, leadership opportunities, and other relevant information.

Organization and Administration

See General Standards

Many models exist for organizing minority student programs and services. The size and philosophy of the institution usually determine its organization. Generally, however, it is recommended that minority student programs and services be organized within student affairs.

Human Resources

See General Standards

It is important that representatives of the various cultures involved be included on the professional staff.

Professional staff should be competent in career planning and development, group facilitation, leadership training and development, workshop design, social-interpersonal development,

and individual and group counseling. Generally, these competencies are found in persons who graduate from student personnel, counseling, or higher education graduate preparation programs.

Specific coursework in the following areas is desirable: organizational development, counseling theory and practice, group dynamics, leadership development, human development, and research and evaluation.

The use of graduate assistants and interns should be encouraged. Such assistants expand staff abilities, provide peer role models, and give valuable preprofessional experience. Particular attention should be given to preparing all preprofessional assistants to be especially sensitive to cultural differences and the special needs of minority students.

Student employees and volunteers from minority groups should be utilized and assigned responsibilities that are within their scope of competence. These paraprofessional helpers should be selected carefully, trained to do their assigned jobs, and supervised by the professional staff on a regular basis.

Funding

See General Standards

It is common in many institutions for some of the programs offered by minority student programs and services to be funded by grant resources. In these cases, the institution should make appropriate efforts to transfer funding from grants to the regular institutional budget when the programs have demonstrated effectiveness and efficiency, and are judged to be valuable.

Facilities

See General Standards

Adequate space should be provided for a resource library, private individual consultations, group workshops, and work area for support staff. Many of the programs offered by minority student programs and services require the same level of privacy as individual and group counseling. It is important, therefore, that the physical facilities be adequate for these purposes.

Campus and Community Relations

See General Standards

Professional staff must coordinate, or where appropriate, collaborate with faculty and other staff in providing services and programs for minority students.

Coordination and collaboration are important in order to minimize isolation of the minority student program and maximize the use of faculty and other staff resources in meeting the needs of minority students.

Ethics

See General Standards

The professional staff must be knowledgeable about the research and practice in areas appropriate to their programming with minority students.

Professional staff must respond in some manner to formal requests by students for personal recommendations.

Recommendations made by staff members should reflect only the professional contacts and observations they have personally experienced with the students.

The use of pejorative stereotypical statements should be carefully avoided.

Professional staff should not initiate formal employment recommendations without the knowledge and consent of the student involved.

Professional staff should inform the student if they cannot make a positive recommendation.

Evaluation

See General Standards

Evaluations should be made on both programs under development and established programs.

Formative and summative evaluations are especially important when the development or operation of a program or service is funded by grants or other "soft" money. Both accountability to the granting agency and establishing a data base for supporting transfer of programs to the general budget require careful evaluation.

General evaluation of the minority student programs and services should be conducted on a regularly scheduled basis. Evaluative data should be solicited from current minority students and alumni who have used the programs or services.

Standards and Guidelines for Minority Student Programs and Services can only be interpreted or applied in conjunction with the General Standards which contain the only reference to certain substantive standards common to all functional areas.

Prepared by the Council for the Advancement of Standards for Student Services/Development Programs, 1986.

Index

A

Academic and career advising, for American Indian students, 70–71

Academic preparation: of American Indian students, 67–68; and black students, 36; and student development model, 13

Activism, for black student services, 32–33

Adams v. Richardson, and black students, 25

Admissions: for Hispanic students, 61; open, and American Indian students, 71; open, and black student services, 34

Africa, and Hispanic students, 51

Aitken, L. P., 67, 78, 99

Alabama, University of, and civil rights movement, 8

Alaska, statehood for, 9

Allen, W. R., 97–98

American Indian Science and Engineering Program, 75

American Indian students: academic preparation of, 67–68; analysis of, 65–79; and civil rights movement, 33; future programs for, 76–78; and Hispanics, 50, 51; history of, 7, 65–66; interventions for development of, 69–76; and opportunity, 6; and persistence, 68; and population increases, 40; profile of, 66–68; recruitment of, 68–69; resources on, 98, 99, 100, 102; and statehood, 9; and student development model, 11, 69–76; summary on, 78; values of, 73–74

American Missionary Association, 24

Aptheker, 25

Arce, J., 25, 94

Arizona, statehood for, 9, 51

Arizona State University, and black students, 6

Arkansas, University of, and civil rights movement, 8

Asante, M. K., 98

Asian American students: analysis of, 39–48; background on, 39–40; and civil rights movement, 33; conclusion on, 48; diversity of, 42–43; as Hispanic, 50; history of, 40, 47–48; and intergroup acceptance, 47–48; and interventions for, 43–47; and opportunity, 6; and population increases, 40; prejudice and discrimination against, 40–41; resources on, 98, 99, 100–101; and student development model, 11; values of, 41–42; and wars, 9–10

Asian American studies, collaboration with, 46

Assimilation, for Hispanic students, 52–53

Association of American Colleges, 91, 93

Astin, A. W., 5, 6, 19, 20, 27, 38, 53, 63, 67, 69, 71, 77, 78

B

Banks, J. A., 84, 85, 86, 93

Barnaart, V., 2–3

Beal, P. E., 54, 63

Beckman, B., 83, 93

Berry, J. W., 52, 63

Black Christians Group, 15

Black students: analysis of, 23–38; and campus environment, 16, 17, 27, 29–30; and civil rights movement, 32, 33; collegiate experience of, 28–30; effective programs for, 35–37; first- and second-generation, 30–31; health and wellness for, 14; as Hispanic, 50; history of, 6–7, 24–26; issues in success of, 26–28; and opportunity, 6; and peer interactions, 83, 91; and population increases, 40; resources for, 37; resources on, 97–98, 99, 101; services for, 31–35; summary on, 37–38; types of services for, 34–35; and wars, 10

114